Clara Fitzroy Kelly Bromley

A Woman's Wanderings in the Western World

A Series of Letters Addressed to Sir Fitzroy Kelly

Clara Fitzroy Kelly Bromley

A Woman's Wanderings in the Western World
A Series of Letters Addressed to Sir Fitzroy Kelly

ISBN/EAN: 9783744713139

Printed in Europe, USA, Canada, Australia, Japan

Cover: Foto ©Thomas Meinert / pixelio.de

More available books at **www.hansebooks.com**

A WOMAN'S WANDERINGS

IN THE

WESTERN WORLD

A Series of Letters addressed to

SIR FITZROY KELLY, M.P.

BY HIS DAUGHTER

MRS. BROMLEY

LONDON

SAUNDERS, OTLEY, AND CO.

66 BROOK STREET, HANOVER SQUARE

1861

THE following pages contain a short narrative of travel in North and South America, Mexico, and the West Indies, undertaken by the Author for the renovation of health and spirits, severely shaken by domestic losses during the preceding year. The author gladly takes this occasion of expressing her grateful sense of the kindness, courtesy, and hospitality she met with from all whom she came across during her tour. It is no small tribute of praise in honour of the Spanish, American, and Spanish-American people, to state the fact, that during a period of ten months' travel in their domains, and over a space of upwards of 20,000 miles, a woman and a stranger, accompanied only by a young friend (a girl), met with no word or act of annoyance from first to last.

WANDERINGS IN THE WESTERN WORLD.

CHAPTER I.

St. Thomas, *July 17th,* 1853.—We arrived here, my dear Father, this morning, after a prosperous and pleasant voyage of fifteen days. I can scarcely persuade myself yet that the past fortnight is not a dream ; that I really am in another hemisphere, and another clime; that the view I am now contemplating of this beautiful island, its deep blue sky and tropical vegetation, will not dissolve itself into the Apsley gardens and the statue of Achilles, or some equally familiar home scene. However, assuming that I am awake, I will, according to promise, note down for your amusement (I hope) during your few hours of leisure, all my doings and adventures in their due course. The first few days after leaving South-

ampton were chiefly occupied in " fixing " ourselves,
and making acquaintance one with another, neither
of which was attended with much difficulty, as fortunately neither Eleanor nor I have suffered at all from
sea-sickness. On the seventh day we sighted the
Azores, especially the island of St. Michael, and were
able just faintly to discern the Peak of Pico. I was
sorry not to be allowed to land; but the rules of the
packet service forbid touching anywhere on the way,
except in a case of necessity. We have had the
advantage of two captains during the voyage, as,
besides Captain Woolley, who commands our beautiful Paranà, we are accompanied by Captain Abbott,
who joins his own ship, which has been out here
under repair. Our fellow-passengers have been
mostly agreeable and kindly-disposed people, gathered
indeed from many different nations. We formed a
miniature Babel between us in point of tongues ; but
luckily there was neither quarrel nor disagreement,
and I believe we shall all part and go on our respective ways now with mutual regret. I must not forget to tell you that I have been persuaded by two or
three experienced travellers in these countries, to
change the route I had originally intended to take,
and instead of paying my visit at Barbados now, and
proceeding to America later in the season, I propose
going at once to Havana, thence make a short tour in
the United States, and return south to Barbados in

October or November. There is some risk, I am
told, of being snowed up and detained for months in
America when travelling so late in the year. . . .
Finding that the Clyde (the steamer bound for
Havana) does not sail till to-morrow at mid-day, we
went on shore this morning, and took a drive about
the town and environs, a friend of Captain Abbott's
having good-naturedly organised a carriage and pair
of horses to be in readiness for us. The yellow fever
is still raging in St. Thomas, I am sorry to hear,
though its violence has much abated during the last
few weeks. It is now chiefly confined to the ships in
the harbour, especially that part where the coaling
takes place; but both town and land are now comparatively free from the scourge. It is singular,
however, that no one speaks of it as a thing they
feared in the least degree. A row of about ten
minutes brought us to the shore, and for the first time
I trod *not* on European ground. St. Thomas is not
generally named as a favourable specimen of a tropical
climate; but it is so new to me, and the change is in
every respect so complete from all we left on the
other side of the Atlantic, as to be sufficient to please
by its novelty alone. What richness of colour per-
vades everything,—land, sea and sky seem to vie with
each other in depth and gorgeousness of hue. At the
risk of horrifying and displeasing my compatriots, for
good and all, I must aver that I never knew before

what *real* green trees and green grass were.   One peculiarity of the vegetation here I cannot understand,
namely, that with a tropical sun absolutely blazing
all day, and with pretty nearly equal violence throughout the year, yet nothing seems burnt; leaves, trees,
and plants look as fresh as spring.   Now in England
or France, or any temperate climate, a fortnight
uninterrupted summer sunshine is enough to burn,
dry up, and change the colour of everything; in
short, the glory of the summer would have departed.
I suppose there must be some way of accounting for
this singularity, but for my part, I must apply to
some wiser head than my own to elucidate it.   There
are palm trees in abundance here, the principal features in all my beau-ideal landscapes.   I observed
in the course of our drive, the banyan, tamarind,
and mango, hitherto only known at home in our hothouses.   I admire the tamarind leaf exceedingly; it
is so graceful.   Also I must not omit mentioning my
introduction to a sugar plantation, which, however,
did not make so pleasing an impression as other new
arborical acquaintances.   They (the sugar canes)
look like a forest of rushes; but the people here tell
me I should wait to see them in flower before pro-
nouncing the fiat of " ugly " upon them. *En revanche*
I may be permitted irrevocably so to designate the
inhabitants, *i. e.* the black people.   I could scarcely
have imagined anything so hideous as a black baby,

and I don't know which was worst, one I saw about
six months old, in *white* swaddling clothes, or another
just able to toddle alone, and who, instead of being
a rosy, dimpled little cherub, as might be expected,
was as black as ink, and, moreover, stark naked.
With the grown-up female population, however, de-
ficiency of dress cannot be complained of; every
colour in the rainbow is pressed into the service,
and generally at the same time—the more the better
they seem to think; yellow, sky-blue and pink seem
the fashionable tints, and dresses are generally worn
flounced up to the waist.   Neither shoes nor stockings are usually worn, except on Sundays to go to
church, and then the former are of white satin!   I
was nearly forgetting to chronicle almost the only remarkable curiosity belonging to this island, namely,
a gigantic cotton tree.   I am afraid to trust my
memory as to its age or size, though both were told
me, but its proportions are most colossal, and the
shapes assumed by its gnarled and twisted branches
are most extraordinary.   The tree, altogether, would
form, in the outline, a very good representation of
the Laocoon magnified a hundred times. . . .
The time had now come to bid farewell to the Paraná
and our ocean friends, which we did with real regret.
A long voyage makes one become quite attached
even to inanimate things : I was really grieved to
quit my little cabin.   There are only four of our old

companions going on with us to Havana, the rest are to scatter themselves far and wide in every direction. St. Thomas is the central spot whence radiate all routes to other parts of the western hemisphere. The Clyde seems quite a nutshell after the Paranà. She is commanded by Captain Wilson, a son of the Bishop of Calcutta. I shall close my letter now, as the mail starts for England very early to-morrow morning.—Ever your affectionate,

C.

ENTRANCE TO HAVANA.

CHAPTER II.

Fonda de los Americanos, Havana. — My dear
Father,—We landed here yesterday, and I resume the
narrative of my progress, although this sea travelling
is such an easy nonchalant sort of life, it makes one
quite idle, but as the weather is somewhat hot I shall
be sorry to leave the sea for the land journey. On
the 19th and 20th we coasted along San Domingo
and Porto Rico, but did not touch at either. Early
in the morning of the 22nd the lighthouse of Havana
was in sight, and at 4 o'clock P.M. we entered the
harbour. I had heard in England that the entrance
to Havana was a scene of all but matchless beauty;
this, however, I think is exaggerated; very beautiful
it truly is, and the immense palm trees fringing its
shore, give it a character peculiarly its own: still I
think the ports of Naples, Genoa, and above all,
Corfu, may successfully vie with it in magnificence of
scenery. We were very nearly being obliged to
limit our acquaintance with Havana to its harbour,
and having to go on, in spite of ourselves, to Vera

Cruz, in consequence of our passport not having been *visé* by the Spanish consul at St. Thomas. The police were inexorable. " We must go on," at least we must not stay. It was in vain we assured them we were not conspirators, or worse still, Americans. We were not *en règle*, that was certain, so we must not remain. As things began now to look serious, I thought it better to try what Senor Isturiz's letters would do; so I sent the one to the Captain-general, writing a note to him myself, at the same time stating the circumstances and our dilemma. In the mean time, awaiting his reply, we went on shore, as that is allowed for transitory passengers. Not a little to my relief, and I must confess to my astonishment, the Spanish ambassador's letter had a most magical effect. To begin with : the Captain-general sent the royal boat to bring us on shore, and finding we had already gone, they took our luggage, consequently there was no custom-house searching, as *on ne touche pas à la Reine* or her conveyances. The next surprise that awaited me was in the shape of an aide-de-camp, dressed in full scarlet and gold (the Spanish uniform is almost the same as our Guards), who came charged with a message to the effect that the Captain-general himself, and all that he had, was at my disposition. This sounds somewhat wonderful to a stranger, but it is nevertheless the general mode of expression used by the Spanish people of all classes.

If you remark on anything belonging to them in terms of praise, they say immediately, " It is yours," or *a su disposicion de usted*: at your disposal. Of course this is not intended to be taken literally, still it is a courteous and kindly phrase. Having replied to the aide-de-camp in as civil English as I could muster, we proceeded, it being now about eight o'clock, to the Plaza d'Armas, a large square, or rather garden, in front of the palace, where we are told a military band plays every night. But we were little prepared for the scene that awaited us. I can liken it to nothing but the last scene of some fairy piece at a play: groups of glorious palm trees standing in bold relief against the glittering starry sky, the moon shedding floods of light on the spray of a fountain playing in the centre of the Plaza; the flowers, the music, and then the women! As if still further to heighten the resemblance to a play, or I should now rather say, to ¯a ballct, the señoras and señoritas were all in full evening costume; wreaths of flowers or jewels worn by all. They sauntered about with the graceful and indolent walk peculiar to the Spanish, and flirting both with their eyes and their fans, in a manner which, had I been a man, must have been highly detrimental to my head or heart, or both. Still I do wish I were either a painter or a poet, that I might at least describe my impression in something better than this.

23rd.—Took a drive this morning in a volante, a
species of carriage peculiar to Havana, a most curious
affair, and difficult to describe.—A cabriolet body,
placed rather low and forward; two gigantic wheels
almost at the back; traces of excessive length termi-
nating with a horse, mounted by a diminutive black
postillion, who is generally equipped either in green
or crimson velvet and large top-boots. These volantes hold two persons, and sometimes three; they
are very comfortable and easy, the seat being so well
poised, and the springs quite elastic. We wandered
about the town looking at the outside of the various
buildings. The Moro, or lighthouse, placed on a steep
rock at the entrance to the harbour, nearly grown
over with the bright flowers and leaves of the cactus,
gives great beauty to the general *coup d'œil* of the
landscape. The palace, the prison, the new opera-
house, called the Tacon, from General Tacon, who
built it during his vice-royalty here; the fort of
Santa Clara, the Paseo or public promenade, and the
cathedral (the burial-place of Christopher Columbus),
were principal points of interest in our drive to-day.
But as at present we are here only *en passant* and
mean to make a longer stay on our return, I shall
reserve till then any more detailed account. On
coming in to dinner I found a note from the Captain-
general, hoping we would do him the honour of
attending the opera at night, and that he would send

his carriage to convey us there at the proper time. Accordingly, at eight o'clock, a very pretty barouche drove up, and this time two aides-de-camp came to escort us, and in about ten minutes we arrived at the Tacon theatre, and were ushered into the royal box. There were two magnificent chairs, or rather thrones, with the crown and arms of Spain carved above each. We were about to seat ourselves in some more humble places, but were told the Captain-general had desired we should fill the seats of honour ; so recollecting Louis XIV.'s lessons on good breeding, on a somewhat similar occasion, I thought it better to do as I was told without further demur, though for a few moments I could not help feeling nervous, as every pair of eyes in the house were turned upon me. Soon, however, I forgot all about myself in wonder and in admiration of this singularly beautiful theatre. All the boxes are open, that is to say, the occupants are seen from head to foot, which, it need not be said, adds much to the fine effect of the whole, the sides and fronts of the boxes being delicately carved in open gold trellis-work.   The ceiling alone is painted, and that very beautifully, and the backs of the boxes are covered with fluted silk and lace draperies.   Wrapped in contemplation of this brilliant scene, I had not heard the door open, and was considerably startled by a voice at my ear announcing the speaker "was at my feet."   I speedily got upon

mine, and made my first reverence to the Captain-
general, and was about *tant bien que mal* to make a
Spanish speech to him, when, to my great relief, he
addressed me in French; so all was plain sailing then.
General Cañedo is a fine soldierly-looking man,
about fifty years of age, not handsome in face (with
the exception of the eyes), but with a kind, benevo-
lent expression, a good voice, and a thorough gentleman, as may be seen at a glance. The opera was
changed after all for a comedy, in consequence of the
illness of one of the singers.

During the week we have passed here whilst waiting the sailing of the steamer, we have gone about
Havana and its environs. The Paseo or Alameda,
the place where the Havanese betake themselves
every evening for riding and driving, reminds me
rather of the Champs Elysées, only here the avenues
and plantations are all of palm trees. About a mile
and a half from the town is a suburb called the
"Cerro," where most of the aristocracy and some of
the merchants have country-houses, or "Quintas," as
they are called. The gardens attached to these
Quintas are delightful—a wilderness of trees, flowers,
and fruit. We passed two or three evenings with the
Captain-general at his Quinta, played billiards, ate
pine apples, and sauntered about the gardens. He
was always good-natured enough to load us with
flowers when we returned, and such beautiful ones.

I, especially, always managed to get a beautiful bunch of stephanotis.

Yesterday morning went to the cathedral to visit the tomb of Christopher Columbus; a plain marble slab, with a short inscription, is all there is to tell of him. I cannot understand how a generous and noble-natured people like the Spanish should have allowed the remains of one to whom they owe so much to lie neglected and almost forgotten. That he should be buried here, in the land he found and won, is right and just, as well as in accordance with his own dying wishes; but where is the sculptured monument? Where the glowing epitaph which should be seen above the grave of Columbus?

CHAPTER III.

August 4th. — We have now been waiting here twelve days for the Isabel Segunda steamer. She arrived at length, and we came on board last night to sleep, as daybreak was the time fixed for sailing this morning. We have a wonderful collection of people, some of them not of the choicest description, and who look very much out of place in the beautiful crimson and gold-decorated saloon, from a corner of which I' am writing to you. The heat is something indescribable, notwithstanding the sea-breeze; and, as you may imagine, there being a bright moonlight, we were glad to remain on deck the greater part of the night, instead of going to the hot, close, little cabin assigned to us for sleeping quarters.

Friday, 5th.—We touched this morning at a place called Key West, for the purpose of taking on board a lot of turtles. Poor things! it is melancholy to see them flapping and floundering about the deck, awaiting their fate and their turn to be converted into soup! Two of our Cuban friends, who are proceeding

to New York direct in the Isabel, wish to persuade
us to do likewise; but this stifling heat is unbearable;
so we shall adhere to our original plan of travelling
there by land from Charleston, of which place we
are just now in sight, so I must go on deck to take
my first look at the continent of America.   .   .   .
The entrance to the harbour is remarkably wide,
about two miles across.   It is formed by the junction
of two rivers, the Ashley and the Cooper, the former
of which is considerably upwards of 6000 feet in
width, and the latter 4000 feet.   The approach and
the crossing of the bar are difficult, and in stormy
weather must be dangerous enough ; shoals and
quicksands abound.   To-day, though perfectly calm
and fine, our boat pitched, and rolled, and whirled
about in the most distracted manner before succeed-
ing in making good her entrance into the port.
Charleston is at present in a very flourishing condition, being the richest as well as the most populous
town, or rather city, I believe it is more correctly
termed, of South Carolina.   Cotton, rice, and tobacco
are the principal products of the state; but of these
the two first form much the larger portion of the
trade carried on.   After taking some dinner at the
hotel, we procured a vehicle (I have yet to learn
what they are termed here, — whether cabs, flies,
coaches, or carriages, but they are not volantes
at all events), in which we proceeded to find out

what we could of the celebrities of the place. The
streets are wide, clean, and airy; the houses not
altogether ugly, in spite of their being made of
red brick. Some handsome public buildings, including the Exchange, City Hall, and Citadel, but
we were most pleased with the public promenade,
which extends for a considerable distance by the
water side, and is thickly planted with trees. From
this spot a very fine view is obtained of the harbour
and forts, and the ocean beyond. Charleston seems
most unusually protected by strong places. If I
remember rightly, we counted four forts indepen-
dently of the citadel. Of these the most famous
and interesting, to us at least, is Fort Moultrie on
Sullivan's Island, very near to the harbour, where
the English under Sir Peter Parker were repulsed
in the War of Independence in 1776. As you may
suppose, we being Englishwomen, were very especially informed of our national defeat. Having
enjoyed our drive very much, we finished off with
going to witness the departure of the Isabel with our
two friends the D——'s on board, continuing their
route to New York. And now, for the first time
since parting from you at Southampton, we are
alone, that is to say, we shall set out on our travels
to-morrow unaccompanied by any one we know or
have ever seen before. I must make this letter
shorter than usual, being a good deal tired by the

heat and crowd on our voyage from Havana, and our departure to-morrow being very matinal. Moreover, the first portion of our journey is to be again aquatic, in accordance with the suggestion and advice of the people here, and we take the steamer to a place called Wilmington.—Yours ever,

C.

CHAPTER IV.

AFTER a long and not over pleasant sea and land
journey from Charleston, we are now, my dear
father, comfortably " located " for the day here,
namely, at Richmond, in a large, cheerful, and, as
we saw it last night on our arrival, brilliantly
lighted hotel. But before saying anything of this
place, I must begin at the beginning, and chronicle
our movements since I last wrote. Our departure
from Charleston did not, for some reason best
known to the powers on board the steamer, take
place till the afternoon, instead of the morning;
the sky was lowering, atmosphere oppressive, and
boat crowded; and to make matters better, when we
had been about four hours at sea, we met with a
Job's comforter, in the shape of the chief engineer
of the vessel, who informed us that the particular
point we were then turning, and which bore the
ominous name of Cape Fear, was the most dangerous
spot on all the southern coast; that the heavy cloud
we saw " looming in the distance," was the probable

forerunner of a squall; also, that a vessel, for which
the one we were on board was a substitute, had been
lost on just such a night as this, on her return
voyage, having previously, however, landed Jenny
Lind in safety on the outward bound trip. Here
was a pretty catalogue of disasters! Decidedly our
friend must have had the mischievous design of
upsetting our nerves : notwithstanding all these black
prognostications, the night passed without any misadventure, and we reached Wilmington yesterday
morning in safety; a busy-looking, commercial town,
but containing nothing worthy of note in other
respects. It owes its rise, if not its existence, to
being the terminus of the immense line of railroad
from north to south of the United States. To make
up for the absence of the threatened gale of wind
at night, the rain poured down with such extreme
violence, that in walking over the short space of
about twenty yards from the landing to the railway
train, where the "cars" were in waiting, we got
completely wet through. The carriages, or cars as
they are called here, differ considerably in their
construction from those on the European railroads.
Each car is of exceeding length, and instead of being
in compartments with doors at the sides, you enter
at the back, and find a lane, on the principle of the
aisle of a church, straight through the centre of the
car, with rows of benches on either side for the

accommodation of the passengers. These benches have
reversible backs; so that you may sit fronting the
engine or not as you prefer.   I am not sure on the
whole that I like these American cars; it seems to
me that you are not sufficiently protected against
the weather ; there are no means of ventilation,
except by keeping the windows open; and this necessarily, of course, let in a quantity of wet in the
beginning of the journey.   By and by as we proceeded the rain ceased, and the sun began absolutely
to *blaze*,—shine is too mild an expression.   The heat
and dust then became insufferable ; added to which,
the ashes and cinders from the engine blew in upon
us in showers, penetrating every nook and corner,
and certainly neither contributing to our comfort
nor cleanliness.   We looked like a set of sweeps
before reaching our journey's end.   In other respects
the regulations are good enough.   The travelling is
fast, very cheap, and lastly, all the people, employés,
and others are kindly and civilly disposed towards
women.   The general aspect of the country we have
traversed is strange and wild.   We have passed over
upwards of 300 miles of one nearly unvaried scene,
trees and water, water and trees.   Every now and
then a small clearance had been made, the stumps
being left, showing where the trees had been; and
two or three houses were built, rarely more; but a
very few years, they tell me, will suffice to convert

these small beginnings into considerable towns. The grand old names belonging to some of these embryo "cities" are at times ludicrous. *Warsaw,* for instance, consists of exactly four houses. I should not omit to mention that the line of railroad I have just been describing is laid along the outskirts or margin of the great morass immortalised by Moore's poetry, called "The Lake of the Dismal Swamp," which will account for the aquatic character of the greater portion of the route. Dismal enough it looked certainly, especially as night drew on. The last cheerful-looking place we saw was called Petersburg, where we stopped for refreshment, a pretty, green-looking spot, and apparently in a thriving condition. About two hours before arriving at Richmond, it being then quite dark, we had to cross, by means of a very long bridge, a dreary marsh or fen water surrounding us on every side, and the extreme distance only bounded by the dark outline of a sombre forest; our train looking like a thread on the waste of waters: the scene was altogether appalling, and greatly relieved I felt when we had safely crossed it. By day, no doubt, it would look less terrible, but the effect at night is by no means pleasant. I had nearly forgotten to tell you of a curious *notice* I saw posted up at the railway station at Wilmington. It purported to state the fares on some short line, I cannot tell what, between Wilmington and whatever

the place may have been.   It ran thus : " Gents and
ladies 75 cents, children and slaves 35 cents ! "   As
you are aware, there is no first or second class in
American travelling.   *Persons*, therefore, are charged
all equally, but children and *slaves* it should appear
do not count.   Richmond, where we arrived at length
last night, is the capital town of Virginia, and is
remarkably picturesque in its general character.
The private houses, as well as many of the public
buildings, are mostly enclosed in ornamental grounds,
planted with shrubs and trees.   These, together with
there being a waterfall in the immediate vicinity,
the falls of the James River, on which the town is
built, combine to render Richmond somewhat more
of a show place than might be expected of a manufacturing town.   We paid a short visit to the capitol,
which stands in the midst of a very tastefully-planted
square or park, serving as a pleasure-ground and
promenade for the public.   Clumps and avenues
of fine trees, with a quantity of grass-plots intersected with paths and gravel-walks.   Inside the
building there stands facing you as you enter the
hall, a well-executed statue of Washington in white
marble.   I do not know the sculptor's name,—indeed,
to tell the truth, I forgot to ask.   There are several
cotton factories here, but the principal source of
industry is tobacco.   About fifty manufactories are
in action at the present moment, each employing

an average of 150 to 200 hands, *black* hands, of course; and I am told that both the population and commercial prosperity of Richmond are steadily increasing every year. To-morrow we proceed northwards, and expect to reach Washington, so I will write no more to you now, but take up my narrative again when our journey thither is accomplished.

CHAPTER V.

August 9th. — Left Richmond at 7 A.M., and after
about five hours in the train, reached a place they
call Aquia Creek, where we embarked on a steamer,
the Baltimore, which conveyed us up the river
Potomac to Washington, a pleasant little voyage;
the banks of the river green and pretty, though
tame. In this part of the United States there is
much resemblance to our counties of Kent and
Surrey. Green fields, orchards, and a kitchen-
gardeny look about the country, added to red brick
houses in the towns, still further increases the likeness. The people, however, are different in almost
every respect. Nothing strikes me more, as an
Englishwoman, than the interest, or as some call
it, the curiosity, displayed by the people here about
the affairs of strangers. They guess, reckon, or
calculate upon all your actions, and even your
motives. Nevertheless, I am never inclined either
to think or treat this inquisitiveness as an imper-
tinence, and, moreover, I do not think they mean

it themselves as such; I believe it arises from their desire to compare themselves, their sayings and doings, with every stranger they come across, and in their anxiety to do this, they occasionally lose sight of the bounds of good breeding. On the other hand we English go into an opposite extreme. The indifference with which we view everybody we do not know, the fright we are in lest we *should* know some one who is not as high up as ourselves in the social scale. And as to asking questions! I suspect if we could, Asmodeus-like, look into the minds of nineteen out of twenty travellers who meet each other at home, their reflexions would run somewhat as follows: "I don't care where you live or what you are, where you come from or where you are going to, and I only hope you are not going to speak to me." But though, as I have said, I do not think the Americans mean rudeness by their curiosity, they are quite the most conceited people possible; their comparisons, which I have before mentioned, are never by any chance turned to their own disadvantage. Whatever the subject, trivial or important, theirs is the victory, "they beat all creation." And yet, until the Americans cure themselves of some of their personal habits, to which it would be disagreeable more particularly to allude, I think they can scarcely be suffered to class themselves among civilised nations, and

c

certainly not among civilised society. I have rarely
seen, on our side of the Atlantic, peasants or artisans
so offensive in their personal actions as I regret to
say those who call themselves American *gentlemen.*
Apropos of peculiarities and habits, I am rather
amused at the announcements printed and hung
up behind all the room doors in the hotels on the
subject of stealing. We must at least give them
credit for the candour with which they acknowledge
their propensities towards thieving or *annexing*, as
I suppose they would call it themselves. You are
solemnly warned by these notices always to lock
your door and remove your key when you leave
the room, "if you wish to avoid being robbed,"
and to bolt your door inside at night "for fear
of night visitors."—To return to our voyage after
this long digression. About fifteen miles below
Washington, we passed Mount Vernon, the residence and burial-place of the patriot. We could
barely distinguish the monument; but the place
seemed very still and well formed for a refuge from
the turmoil of public life.

August 10*th.*—I forget what author remarks on
Washington, that "it is a city of magnificent in-
tentions." The expression is very well chosen. It
might be, and should the day ever dawn on its
entire completion, it will be most splendid. Seen
from a little distance few towns in the world could

compare with it, but on a near view the charm dis-
solves. Everything is being built, nothing finished;
and even those buildings which to all appearance
are complete and unexceptionable, do not satisfy
the prevailing mania. They will not let well alone,
but must be ever altering, enlarging, *improving*,
and what not, until the whole place resembles a
stone-mason's yard, instead of the metropolis of a
state, and the seat of its government. The capitol
is a most magnificent structure, and might very
well vie with the architectural *chefs-d'œuvre* of
Rome or Athens, were it only left in peace. But
they must " go ahead," and accordingly have begun
to build two wings, which will not, I think, improve
the original design ; and, *en attendant*, obliges one
to wade through stones, dust, and marble on every
side. The interior of the capitol is very simple,
the only ornamental part being immediately under
the dome, which is used apparently as a sort of
lobby by the members of Congress between the
acts of their debates. This dome is hung round
with pictures, by American artists, of the principal
events in their country's history. They include
the baptism of Pocahontas, the discovery of America
by Christopher Columbus, and the landing of the
Pilgrim Fathers. The rest are devoted to the
various memorable episodes in the life of George
Washington. Of these the most remarkable and

the most frequently repeated on their canvass are
those occasions on which the enemy surrendered to
him.   From the summit of the steps of the capitol,
and at the end of a long avenue of noble trees,
is seen the colossal statue of Washington, with the
following short but graceful inscription on the
pedestal: " George Washington, the first in peace,
the first in war, and the first in the hearts of his
countrymen."   Taken as a whole, the effect of
this is very fine, the charming scenery of the back-
ground, the windings of the Potomac, the fine
old trees which completely screen the city from
view, all unite to give the capitol an air of solitary
grandeur.   The Post-office, the Treasury, the President's house, and the Patent-office are each and
all superb buildings, seen from a little distance,
as we did in taking a carriage drive round the
environs.   The impression given by this distant
view is that Washington is one of the most splendid
towns in the world; but alas! the illusion is soon
dispelled.   The buildings are there, certainly, but
not one of them is finished; the streets are laid
out and *named* with the most ludicrous regularity,
but for the most part are guiltless of houses.   Brick-
dust, stone-dust, and marble-dust nearly suffocate
you at every step, besides being lamed in stumbling
over stones and splinters of every description in your
path.   A memorial has been begun to be erected

to Washington, and all the states of the Union
contribute something to it in the shape of a piece
of sculptured marble.   Each piece is to be employed
and placed somewhere when the whole is completed;
but when will that be, I wonder?   The people themselves give half a century before they expect its
completion.   The worst of it is, judging from the
model, I think it will be but an ugly affair after
all.   The drawing resembles a large manufacturing
chimney.   We returned to our hotel (Brown's, Pen-
sylvania Avenue) tired and almost bewildered with
our wanderings about.   How wonderfully cheap,
and generally speaking, how very good the American
hotels are!   This one we are at, for instance, we
have two very nice rooms, drawing-room and bed-
room; the meals are breakfast, dinner, tea, and
supper, all of which are plentifully supplied with
the best food and a great variety, and for which
everything, light and all included, the charge is
a dollar and a half each per diem.   They give you
a *menu* when you come down to breakfast of
the morning's provision,— eggs, omelettes, kidneys,
" chicken-fixings," cutlets, mushrooms, are the usual
items from which you select what you like.   Then
there is an endless variety of bread made of Indian
corn, hominy, and other sorts of grain, but I cannot,
at least yet, like any of these, they are so very heavy,
so I generally adhere to buttered toast, which they

c 3

do to perfection. As I am about to proceed to supper, the long drive having made me remarkably hungry, I shall resume my letter to-morrow, after having visited some more of the Washington objects of interest.

This morning was occupied in the inspection of several of the public buildings of which we had only seen the exterior yesterday. These were the Patent-office, the Post-office, the Smithsonian Institute, and the President's house. The Patent-office is really a noble building, and fortunately it is not only finished, but speaking comparatively, it may almost be termed an ancient structure. It was one of the very few, indeed I believe it was the only one, of the great institutions which escaped destruction in 1814, when our English general Ross, by his famous *coup-de-main*, marched upon Washington, and before the surprised enemy could offer any effectual resistance, had set fire to the capitol, including its library, the docks, the Treasury, the President's abode, the war-office, a great bridge, and two or three ships of war,—a pretty good day's work ! But the Patent-office, as I have said, escaped the general conflagration, owing, they say, to the strong intercession of its then director. The building is of white marble, and in the Italian style of architecture. One very beautiful room, which is devoted to the reception of the various inventions for which patents have been obtained, is upwards of 120 feet long, and is adorned with a double row of marble columns, supporting an arched roof finely sculptured with bas-reliefs. From this we went to the Post-office, also a handsome marble structure, and thence to the President's, called also the "white house." The congress not being in session now, both this and the capitol are deserted, so that one may roam over them at pleasure. The white house is singularly simple and unpretending in its interior decoration, certainly it cannot fairly be termed a palace, and it is scarcely equal to a tolerably well-appointed private abode. Before leaving this part of the city we visited the Congress library, which we had not entered previously. It is in one wing of the capitol, and contains 28,000 volumes. We closed our peregrinations by the inspection of the Smithsonian Institute, one of the many examples of private benevolence and liberality abounding throughout the States. It is a curious and picturesque-looking building of a red granite and in the old turretted style of architecture. It has ten towers, one in the centre much higher than the others. We were not, however, admitted beyond the grounds, a lecture being in course of delivery. As perhaps I shall have no other opportunity of despatching a letter before arriving at New York, I shall send this off to-night, for " *I calculate* " it

will just catch the English mail. It would amuse
you to hear how beautifully E —— imitates the
Yankee twang. I am not so clever at it by a long
way, but with her it sounds quite *genuine*. Adios.

Ever your affectionate

C.

CHAPTER VI.

Baltimore, August 16th. — My dear Father, — We
came here yesterday afternoon, in about an hour and
a half from Washington.   The country through which
we passed was very beautiful, and I should have
admired it still more but that I thought once or
twice we were going to "eternal smash," as they say
here.   We travelled much faster than I ever recollect
doing in England, and frequently far too rapidly to be
safe.   The distance between Washington and Baltimore is but forty miles, and an hour and a half for traversing that space would have been moderate enough,
but a very considerable delay took place at a station
called Annapolis, and then I suppose to make up lee
way they found it necessary to go like "greased lightning !"   What immoderate water-drinkers the Americans are !   There is water in the trains, water
in the boats, water in the railway-stations, water
in the drawing-rooms, and to make matters worse,
at dinner (I am speaking of the table d'hôte dinners
on the road), instead of taking a little wine or beer,

c 5

like people in general, they drink oceans of milk diluted with water. It is to me most unpleasant to look at, especially when accompanying rich entrées and sauces, not to speak of fat pork, which is also a very favourite dish, but does not in my opinion look at all agreeable in juxtaposition with a great tumbler of milk. As we hear that Baltimore does not offer many attractions to a casual visitor, we are enjoying a quiet morning. I can quite appreciate the feeling of some traveller I have read of, who on arriving I forget where, thanked heaven there was nothing to be seen. In a hurried journey one gets sadly tired of lionising. Besides I cannot but feel the almost impossibility of giving any original remarks, or of telling you or any one else anything which you have not repeatedly heard before, though may be in varied forms, about the United States. I take it there is no other country in the world that has been so often, so thoroughly, and so well delineated as this, not even Italy. . . .

Since writing the above we have been out, and I am sorry to say there is more to see than I anticipated. Joking apart, however, there are some memorials of the past peculiarly interesting to English people. The town itself is pretty nearly what I expected, busy and commercial; red-brick houses, and no end of factories and smoke. But besides all this there are some famous monuments. I should mention perhaps that Baltimore is called, *par excellence*, "the monumental city." First, and principally, there is a very fine one in honour of Washington, a Doric column, 160 feet high, surmounted by his statue. It is a magnificent structure, and I think far superior to that in the city of Washington. Another, called Battle Monument, is erected to the memory of the defenders of the city in that same year, 1814, when the English, after the cruel havoc they had made at Washington, essayed a like exploit here, but were repulsed after bombarding the fort (Henry) for twenty-four hours. The unfortunate General Ross, who commanded the English land troops, was killed in the *mêlée*, and the fleet (consisting of sixteen ships), under Admiral Cochrane, was also compelled to retire. The third and last trophy I need mention, is a monument in honour of Colonel Armistead, the American Commander, and is in the form of a pyramid made with cannon, and surmounted with shot and shells. I forgot to tell you that we are located at a hotel yclept "Barnums." I am quite curious to know whether the proprietor is any relation to the famous manager of that name. We purpose, for a change, as the weather is so fine, leaving here at seven this evening, taking a moonlight flitting. The train ought to reach Philadelphia at midnight, and as the moon is now about the full, and gloriously bright, I think it will be a good opportunity of seeing

some American scenery under a fresh aspect. . . .
Nous voici safely deposited in the very middle of the
Quaker city, at the Girard House, a most magnificent
looking hotel at all events.   The nocturnal journey
turned out well, and as I expected, the beautiful
moonlight gave a romantic tint to all it shone upon,
in spite of the prosy squeaking engine and the lumbering cars.   The passage of the River Schuylkill
(what a name!), a little before entering the town,
was an especially picturesque incident.   Philadelphia
is generally called the " prettiest city in the States,"
on what grounds I cannot imagine, unless beauty is
supposed to consist in the most painfully straight
lines and acute angles.   Judging from the aspect
of the town in this morning's perambulation, I
think it probable I should expire of ennui in a
week if forced to stay.   I must endeavour to describe
its general appearance, however, in order that you
may form your own opinion, as may be, my artistic
dislike to extreme regularity renders me unduly pre-
judiced.   So, first of all, there are two rivers : the
before-mentioned unpronounceable Schuylkill, and
the Delaware.   Well, nature made them, so they are
not quite straight.   The city is built between them,
and I cannot liken the long undeviating rows into
which the streets are sliced, to anything better than
the bars of a gridiron, so formal, so guiltless of a
curve.   There are many jokes flying about at the ex-

pense of the prim and precise Philadelphians ; among
others it is said that owing to their excessive correct-
ness they object to resort to the usual and more simple formula of language generally employed, but that
if you ask your way of a passer-by, you will be directed to take the third turning towards the east,
thence proceed due north, whence the place you seek
will be found to your south-west.   Or perchance at
dinner you may be requested to hand the pickled
cucumbers that lie on the south-east of the stewed
ham; or the dish of Indian corn to the north-west of
the pumpkin pie!

There are several squares here which are pretty
enough, and like most of these enclosures in the
towns of the United States, tastefully laid out with
trees, shrubs and walks.   Independence Square we
especially visited as being the spot on which the
American declaration of Independence was pro-
claimed.   The room in the State House hard by,
where the document was finally agreed upon and
signed on the memorable 4th of July, is still left as it
was in every respect, as a memento of the deed.   On
leaving the State House we proceeded to the Fairmount waterworks, a pleasant drive of about three
miles from the town.   The water (to the amount of
22,000,000 gallons) is kept in four reservoirs on the
top of a mount or mound of earth 100 feet high, to
which it is raised by mechanical power from the river

beneath. The reservoirs are surrounded and the
mount intersected with gravel walks and paths,
shaded by chesnut trees and evergreen shrubs, forming a cool and agreeable promenade in summer
weather, and the eminence, though slight in itself, is
sufficient to afford a good and extensive view both of
town and country, all being so flat for many miles
round.   The cost of these works came to 450,000
dollars, about 90,000l.; and I was told that upwards
of a hundred miles of iron piping is used in conveying the water from the Fairmount to and through all
the various quarters of the city.   The Girard College,
to which our steps were now directed, is a large stone
building, on the model of the Parthenon at Athens,
but it is a poor imitation of the original in point of
architecture.   The object of the institution is a most
praiseworthy one.   A large sum of money—I believe
200,000 dollars—was left to the city of Philadelphia
by a Frenchman of the name of Girard, for the purpose of building a college for the education of orphan
boys.   The pupils are received between the ages of
eight and eighteen.   We were shown all over the
building, as well as the grounds and gardens, which
are extensive and handsome.   The officials were particularly civil and good-natured in replying to all our
questions.   The organisation of the establishment is
carried on in the most liberal and generous scale, and

in the way of learning, the students are taught everything they may wish to know.

There is much in the domestic manners and customs in this country to which I find it impossible to reconcile myself. When will the people learn that they may be free and independent yet at the same time neither coarse nor vulgar? An incident occurred to-day at dinner, at which I cannot help laughing, though I was excessively irritated. Among other singularities to which I cannot subscribe, is that of rushing in at the sound of the dinner-bell, like so many wild beasts going to feed; and then when they are there, the way they bolt everything, seize everything, and heap everything eatable on their plates at once, as if they feared their neighbours would *annex* their share. I was walking at my usual pace along the dinner room, about two minutes after the bell had ceased ringing, and looking for my seat, when suddenly two hands (from behind) were placed on my shoulders, and the voice of a waiter, with the most shocking twang, thus addressed me:—"Well, *Miss*, I calculate if you want *victuals* you had better go a-head!" Altogether, this hotel has by no means tended to improve my impression of the inhabitants of this, undeniably, "first-rate" country (to use their own favourite expression). At night we had another sample of their *equality*, and for the first time, I must

observe also, I found a want of the usual courtesy to
our sex, though to be sure the offender was only a
boy.   On reaching our bed-room we found darkness
instead of the gas we expected, and we had omitted
to provide or indeed think of bringing a light
with us.   We rang the bell and asked for a candle,
when our waiter, an urchin apparently not more
than thirteen or fourteen, after putting his arms a-
kimbo and *spitting* on the floor, told us he "guessed
we might fetch one for ourselves, as we ought to have
brought one up with us."

We leave Philadelphia to-morrow; and as I find my
letter has already expanded itself considerably, I will
defer to my next our journey to New York.

Always, &c.

C.

CHAPTER VII.

New York, August 22nd. — My dear Father, — We quitted Philadelphia early in the morning of the 20th, that is, the day before yesterday, a short railway journey of about sixty miles brought us to Amboy, not a very interesting route ; the country flat and sandy. The only object of note we passed was at Bordentown, where the house and grounds formerly occupied by Joseph Buonaparte were pointed out to us. Amboy is situated at the extremity of a creek or arm of the sea running inland. Here we left the cars and embarked in a steamer. It is pleasant to be able to praise something ; so as to make up for all the wrath and indignation poured forth in my last letter to you about Philadelphia. I must frankly allow that the first view of New York far surpasses in splendour any town in the world I have yet seen, and of those the number is not small. Everything which constitutes either magnificence or beauty seems united here. Sea and river, mountain and garden, houses, ships, trees, all seem to vie with each

other in adding to the charm of this matchless scene,
coloured too as it was by the light of the setting sun.
I can scarcely imagine anything more beautiful than
the view which burst upon us as we gradually approached the entrance to the harbour.   The channel
narrowing and disclosing Staten Island with its green
trees and bright-hued gardens on the one side, and
the fine suburb of New Jersey, apparently itself
a city of palaces on the other.   It is said that the
united navies of the whole world would have room to
float in the New York waters.   Whether this may be
an exaggeration or not I am not competent to decide;
but the idea of great space and vastness must strike
the most casual observer.·   Judging from the impressions of the first four-and-twenty hours, I am inclined
to give this the preference over any of the towns
I have yet visited in the States.   It is bustling and
noisy to be sure; still it is cheerful, and I should
think agreeable as a residence.   The far-famed and
world-renowned " Broadway," *the street* par excellence of New York, I am almost afraid to mention.
It has been so written to death by travellers of every
kind, still it is unavoidable.   " Broadway " is the
"Canebière" * of New York.   As far as I can see
at present, all the shops, or *stores,* as they call them,

---

* In allusion to La Canebière, a famous street in Marseilles, concerning which the Provençal people are in the habit of observing,
" Que si Paris avait la Canebière, ce serait un petit Marseille ! "

in the town, seem to be accumulated here; as well
as the greater number of the hotels. These last-
mentioned establishments are almost the distinctive
feature of the place. Public or national buildings, so
to speak, exist in very small numbers; but the hotels
are magnificent beyond all conception,— palaces
indeed they may be rather called, both in size and
redundancy of ornament. They are for the most part
built either of pure white marble or of a reddish-
brown granite, the latter in my opinion especially
beautiful. Attached to Broadway towards the higher
part of it are several very fine streets consisting
entirely of private houses. These streets are mostly
called " Avenues," and are numbered " 4th, 5th,"
&c. They are chiefly inhabited by the " upper ten
thousand." . . . . The place of our disem-
barcation on Saturday presents a curious example
of the different purposes to which things in this
world may be applied. The spot is named indifferently, the Battery or the Castle Gardens, and one
of its uses is that of a general landing-place for
voyagers coming from or going to the south. Being
well laid out in shady walks, planted with trees
and shrubs, it forms a pleasant rendezvous where
you may meet your friends. Indeed, it is the only
thing of the kind in New York, bearing the remotest
resemblance to one of our parks. But besides all
this, there is something else, and at night the scene

changes—into what should you guess? No less an
institution than the Italian Opera! called, for the
nonce, the Castle Garden Theatre. The ancient
name of Castle Garden was Castle Clinton, erected
as one of the defences of the harbour; but as time
went on and new and more efficient fortifications
were built, this was turned to the pacific purpose
of a place of public amusement; and finally, as I
have said, it is now used as the Italian Opera House.
Not feeling by any means fatigued, we went there
on the evening of our arrival. The interior is quite
different from the general notion one entertains of
an Opera House. There are no boxes at all; the
world sits in what we should call the pit; ladies wear
bonnets, and gentlemen what they please. Sontag*
is the prima donna at present, and took the part of
Rosina in the Barbiere; but either she is not in
good voice, or else she is *saving* it. Knowing her
style so well as I do, I could see there was something not right. She gave the impression of a
person humming or trying over a song before proceeding to perform it properly . . . I now resume my letter after a *relache* of two or three days,
employed chiefly in reading your budget from
England. We have been to church, and also to a place
of musical entertainment called Christy's Minstrels;

* Poor Sontag died, in Mexico, of cholera nine months afterwards.

the former I should not mention, but that the Divine Service took place at Trinity Church, the principal and handsomest church, not only in New York, but I believe I might add in the United States, which are sadly deficient in church architecture. There is nothing whatever in any of the American churches, I have seen, either to please the eye or ear. This Trinity is Gothic, spacious, and possesses a very high steeple ; but I think that is all. Christy's Minstrels are amusing enough. They are a set of apparently black men, numbering from twelve to fourteen persons, and who impersonate the " darkies;" talk as they talk, sing as they sing, and play the banjo, *bones* and other instruments. They perform alternately solos, duets, trios and choruses. Some of the airs are exceedingly melodious, and the words adapted to them quite pathetic. Two especially I noted are most touching called " Old Dog Tray," and " My old Kentucky Home, Good Night." We went this afternoon to dine with Mr. K. the banker, to whom I had a letter of introduction. His country residence is at Hoboken, a suburb of New York about five miles off. The scenery on the way was beautiful and moreover quite wild. It is difficult to believe that so large a city is close at hand, one might fancy oneself hundreds of miles afar in the backwoods, so still and silent. We dined with Mrs. K.'s family. They have a pretty house and grounds, with a magnificent view from their garden, of New York in the distance, and the Hudson flowing at their feet. Mrs. K. and the daughters are hospitable, amiable people, with lovely faces like all American women.

N.B. — The driver missed his way in returning, and we did not get back till late.

CHAPTER VIII.

August 25th. — Set out last evening by the light of a bright moon, *en route* to Niagara.   The railroad for some distance was along the banks of the Hudson, which are very beautiful by day and may be called *romantic* by night.   I intend, if all be well, to return to New York by boat on the river, and thus to see the beauties of the road by land and water. Reached Niagara early this morning and proceeded immediately across the river to the Clifton House on the Canadian side.   The view of the falls being better in every respect here than on the American shore.   I know it is the fashion with most people to go almost out of their senses on the first view of the Niagara, or at the very least to be rendered speechless, entranced, and what not at the first introduction to the falls.   I regret to be obliged to confess that no such violent effect has been produced on my hardened nerves, and yet I do think them glorious, and though not *astonished*, on the other hand, I am not disappointed.   There is one peculiarity in these falls which is unaccountable, that is, that barring the noise, you can form a perfectly correct estimate of the appearance of them from pictures, even indifferent ones.   This is very singular, as generally speaking, falling water is precisely the thing painting can rarely render natural, yet in this instance there is an exception.   The American Falls are just opposite my windows, the larger one, called the Horse-shoe, a little further on in the distance. Took a short walk to the far-famed Table-rock in the afternoon, from the brink of which the Horse-shoe Fall is seen in all its splendour.

29th.—Crossed to the American side by a suspension bridge (something like the one at Friburg, but not so fine), and went to Goat Island, whence we saw the *rapids* to perfection.   Then, after some considerable clambering and climbing, slipping and sliding, we made our way down nearly underneath the American Fall.   We were speedily enveloped in the mist and spray, and, as may be supposed, nearly deafened by the roar.   Having sufficiently gazed from below, we proceeded to re-ascend our difficult path.   At length we reached the summit, and then drove along the shore to the rapids.   A little round tower like a lighthouse has been constructed in the middle of the river, and is approached by means of a bridge made of the trunks of trees.   The tower is built as near as safety will allow to the edge of the cataract.

30th.—Embarked this morning in a steamer bearing the romantic name of The Maid of the Mist. Her travelling experiences have been few, as she was built on the spot. She takes the same short voyage three times every day, and is moored for the night at the place of her birth. She goes bravely through her task notwithstanding; passing under and through the torrent and mist of the American Falls, and as close as prudence permits to the Horse-shoe, which is by no means so placable as its neighbour, and obliges one to keep at a very respectful distance. What has charmed me most in our excursion to-day has been the number and variety of rainbows : of all hues and in every conceivable spot near the falls; now arching over them, now dipping under them, now shooting across, and occasionally forming a complete circle. Spent the rest of the morning in Goat Island, a delightful lounging-place, with every charm that nature can give around you. I should not greatly object to pitching my tent permanently at Niagara. We reserve for this afternoon the bouquet of our Niagara expedition, if such a term may be used, applied to *water* as well as fire-works. It consists in what is called going under the Horse-shoe Fall. Having been ushered into a small dressing-room, we were provided with the *costume de rigueur* on such occasions : a pair of drawers and stockings of flannel, then a pair of trowsers and a dress of bloomer fashion,

D

descending only to the knees, both made of india-
rubber, and lastly, a covering for the head of an indescribable shape, something between a quakeress's
bonnet and a helmet.   Thus elegantly equipped we
started, accompanied by four guides.   Presently we
came to a sort of shelf or ledge cut out of the rock, a
most slippery place, and it was with great difficulty
we could keep our footing.   Along this we proceeded
for some hundred yards or thereabouts, until we
found ourselves completely underneath, and in the
hollow of the arch formed by the leap of the immense body of water from the rock above us.   The
scene here was terrific, and rather calculated to shake
one's courage. The noise was awful! added to which,
the blinding spray from the whirlpool boiling and
foaming below quite frustrated any attempt at using
our eyes, besides finding it very difficult to preserve
our equilibrium.   At length we emerged in safety, but
drenched to the skin, notwithstanding our india-
rubber preservatives.

31st.—A comparatively idle morning passed in
my favourite nook on Goat Island.   One might
dream away one's existence very pleasantly here.
The hand of man has fortunately left nature alone
in her grandeur.   The fine forest spreads its dark
masses far and wide undisturbed, and above all un-
improved by mortal touch.   The stillness which
perhaps might otherwise be oppressive, being broken

by the roar of the falling water, and the fluttering of innumerable birds of a most brilliant orange colour, who appear to have chosen this spot as their home. As we were slowly wending our way back to the Clifton House, we found ourselves in the midst of a very unexpected scene of excitement. A slave had escaped from the American side of the Niagara, and had already swum nearly half-way across; his pursuers were frantically pushing off a boat; the suspense then became painful, I have hardly yet recovered my breath; but it was all right at last, though a narrow escape—the fugitive gained the Canadian shore, and he was safe. I could not find out whether he had been guilty of anything more than running away. Very probably he had, and I have not the slightest doubt he deserved to have been caught; still my sympathies are always with the hunted and not with the hunters, under any circumstances. After dinner we took a drive to the village of Chipewa, an Indian settlement on the banks of the Niagara River, and also the scene of one of the many fights between the Americans and ourselves during the war. It is now a quiet thriving little place, where the Indians bring the specimens of their handiwork for exhibition and sale to the numerous visitors constantly passing to and fro. We made several purchases of them. Their embroidery is exceedingly pretty: shoes, card-cases, boxes made of the skin and worked with the hair of the Moose-deer, ingeniously dyed to the required tints of the flowers or fruit it is worked to represent. Also they make fans, screens, and other ornaments of eagles' feathers in a most admirable manner.

CHAPTER IX.

September 2nd.—We are once more on the waste
of waters : out of sight of land, somewhere about the
middle of Lake Ontario; so before we leave the
steamer, which we expect to do to-night, and consequently will have fresh matter to relate, I will take
up the thread of my narrative from the time of
leaving Niagara. You will have observed that while
there I adopted the diary form, wishing to note down
the impressions of the moment. We took our departure from the Clifton House yesterday morning.
A drive of eight miles on a tram-road brought us to
Queenstown, where we crossed the Niagara by means
of the suspension bridge, to Lewiston. This bridge is
said to be the largest in the world, but it does not
appear to me to be so wide nor so high as that at
Friburg; its length is 1040 feet. From the heights
above this town a most charming view is obtained of
the valley of Niagara and Lake Ontario. Here, too,
there was a very sanguinary engagement, in 1812,
between the United States and British forces, in

which the English General, Brock, was killed. A
column has been erected to his memory, but some
years ago it was blown up in the middle of the night
by some envious American. A good deal of it was
destroyed, and it looks now in a very shattered condition. Some years ago there was an attempt made
to restore it, but this has been abandoned.—*Apropos* of envy and jealousy, I forgot to mention that
while at Niagara Falls, during one of our excursions,
the spot was shown to us where, according to our
guide, one of the "decisive battles of the world" was
fought, and at which I need not say the English were
entirely defeated.—Lundy's Lane was the name of
the battle-field. After a short delay at Lewiston we
embarked on one of the largest and most magnificent
steam-boats imaginable (whence I am now writing).
It resembles a floating castle more than a ship, with
highly ornamented saloons and cabins built on deck;
the roofs of these again being carpeted so as to form
a place for walking; the whole surmounted by an
awning during the sunshiny hours. A little before
sunset we reached Toronto. Here we remained some
hours, but not having any introductions to any of the
inhabitants, I did not think it worth while to land, so
contented myself with its external appearance, which
is very handsome : houses and streets are large and
well-built. I am told its population has exactly
doubled itself in the past ten years. I

have just met with a curious interruption, which I will relate whilst the recollection of it is fresh on my mind. A party of young girls, numbering about six or seven, walked up to the table at which I am writing, and after a moment's pause thus addressed me, " Miss ! Tell me now, where were you educated ?" I certainly have seldom been more taken aback than at this sudden query, for I feared I had unintentionally offended some one, though in what way I was totally ignorant. However, I thought the simple truth would be the best reply, so I answered, " Partly in England, partly in France." The riddle was now soon solved : it appears that when we first came on board yesterday, they heard Eleanor and me talking French together, as we very frequently do, consequently we were set down as French ; but this morning, on finding us equally familiar with the English tongue, they determined to resolve their doubts then and there, and so took this singular method of doing so. We have now had a very amicable conversation, and have given each other some mutual information about the manners and customs of our respective countries. They are travelling in a party of eight, and are about to make a vacation tour in Canada. Though to us it seems strange, it is quite a common practice here for a lot of school girls to join together on the breaking up of the colleges and schools, and make a summer holiday trip wherever they may feel inclined, and unchaperoned by fathers, mothers, or governesses. Last night, towards twelve o'clock, there appeared a very beautiful aurora borealis, which illuminated the heavens in a wondrous manner. We are just now arriving at Kingston, where I believe there will be a change of steam-boats; the colossal affair we are now in not being adapted to some of the narrow channels through which we shall have to thread to-morrow. So adieu for the present: my next will probably be from Montreal.

Always your affectionate

C.

Since writing the above I find we are to anchor here for the night, and take the other steamer to-morrow: plenty of daylight being necessary during the passage of the St. Lawrence.

CHAPTER X.

MY DEAR FATHER,—At an early hour of the morning after our arrival at Kingston we commenced our voyage down the river St. Lawrence. In about a couple of hours we came to the "Thousand Isles," a numerous group so called, among which we threaded our way for some time. These islets are very celebrated for their beauty, though, individually, I should call them more curious than picturesque; moreover, some of them are really too small to be dignified by the name of islands, being merely little beds of earth. Indeed, the whole collection conveys the idea of having once been a good-sized piece of land, now broken into a number of small portions and tossed into the water. The surrounding scenery on the green banks of the St. Lawrence is, however, very pleasant to look upon. The navigation of the rapids, a little below the "Thousand Isles," now engaged our attention. They are very dangerous, and require, even in a steam-boat, most careful management. The river rushes along most furiously, and all

around, in most unpleasant propinquity, rise huge
rocks, threatening destruction to all who approach
them, and against any one of which, had we struck,
we must have gone to pieces and probably perished in
a moment. We fortunately, however, had a steady
and skilful commander, and in due time we were
clear of all difficulties. Near these rapids, by the
bye, is laid the scene of the famous Canadian boat-
song, " Row, brothers, row." The singers were in
ancient days the fur traders of Montreal, who were in
the habit of ascending the Ottawa River, which is
just above these rapids, to sell their goods to the Indians. They used to stop at a church on an island
dedicated to Saint Ann, their tutelary saint, and offer
their orisons to her : hence the allusion you will
remember in the song: " We'll raise to St. Ann," &c.
A pleasant sail for two or three hours more brought
us to Montreal, the first impression of which is most
agreeable. I was quite rejoiced to see the English
flag flying once more.   Not that it can be compared
in point of beauty to the stars and stripes; still it is
more comfortable to see the English flag where you
hear the English tongue. Having established ourselves in the best quarters we could find at Done-
gana's Hotel, Montreal being at present very crowded,
we proceeded to employ the remaining hour or two
of daylight in reconnoitring the town and neighbourhood. The scenery I find remarkably pretty, and,

moreover, the city has an air of comfort, and to a certain extent of antiquity, rarely to be seen in the States.
We drove for a short distance along the base of the
Montreal Mountain, as it is called *par excellence*, and
then made the ascent.   The view from its summit
is most picturesque,—green undulating land dotted
with country houses and cottages, with beautiful gardens and trees.   This morning we visited the Cathedral, and one or two other churches, but they are in
nowise remarkable, at least they look paltry after the
splendour of the Catholic churches in Europe.   The
scene of the terrible fire which occurred here three
years ago was pointed out to us.   It has fearfully devastated a great part of the town.   It seems difficult
to understand how such a fire could have lasted so
long a time and have done so much mischief, as the
houses were not built of wood, which I had always
imagined to be the case ; yet the flames raged and
raged on in spite of every effort, and for some time
burst forth again and .again, notwithstanding several
houses being blown up in order to create a blank
space and check the progress of the conflagration.
We went also to visit a convent belonging to the
order of *Les Sœurs Grises*.   There are, I believe, a
great number of religious houses of this description
in Montreal.   These sisters do much good in the
town, attending the sick, comforting the unhappy,
and besides they take a number of children, orphans,

foundlings, and others, whom they feed, clothe, and educate. We visited the various rooms and saw the children at their different occupations. They all looked both healthy and happy. Having seen all that was worthy of especial note down below, including a most beautiful and wonderful garden, belonging to a Montreal merchant, whose name I forget, but who has collected here everything which is rich and rare, in shrub or flower, we proceeded to drive up the Mountain again, to see what used to be the governor of Canada's country residence, but which is now turned into a sort of *café* where you eat ices, lunch, &c. The house is handsome, and the view all round exceedingly fine. Lord Elgin used to stay here a good deal, but since the riots which took place some time ago, on the subject of the Rebels Indemnity Bill, as I think it was called, the seat of government has been transferred to Quebec; and although Lord E. has been repeatedly entreated to return to Montreal, he has refused. I hear they treated him with great indignity and acted very disgracefully. Our driver gave us a very amusing account of the proceedings on that memorable day. From an early hour in the morning every one who possessed any eggs was waylaid, and their eggs bought for whatever they chose to ask, but if they refused to sell they were taken from them by force; and thus armed they awaited Lord Elgin's sortie, when imme-

MONTREAL — QUEBEC — HEIGHTS OF ABRAHAM. 61

diately he appeared the signal was given, and from
far and near, from right and left, from above and below, came the shower of eggs. Though rather ludicrous, after all it was excessively insulting, and I
don't wonder at his refusal to take up his abode with
such hosts. ˙ The grievance complained of was, that
by this obnoxious bill the innocent and loyal subjects
who had made no disturbance were taxed, or in some
way made to pay, for repairing the damage done to
property by the insurgents. This does seem rather
hard certainly. However, I am only able to relate
one side, so of course can form no opinion on the real
merits of either. The chief cause of complaint
against Lord Elgin was, that although he knew how
very objectionable and unpopular this measure was,
he did not even try to throw the responsibility off his
own shoulders, which he might have done, by sending
it to England for approval, but, on the contrary, took
it all on himself and signed it. We returned, shortly
after hearing all this, to our hotel. At 6 P.M. we left
in the Countess of Elgin steamer, for Quebec, where
we landed on Sunday morning, 4th September. The
harbour and shipping; the old-fashioned houses clus-
tered one above another up the steep hill-side; the
beautiful St. Lawrence; and lastly, the renowned
heights of Abraham frowning above all, give Quebec
a most imposing appearance. Our eyes were still
further gladdened by the sight of red coats on landing,

and our ears by the merry sound of the bugle calling
our own regiments to parade.

Now I shall despatch this at once, and give Quebec
a letter to itself: till when good bye.

Ever yours,

C.

CHAPTER XI.

Russell's Hotel, Quebec, September 5th. — My dear Father,—If I remember rightly, my last letter was closed at the moment of our arrival at Quebec. With as little delay as possible, our time of sojourn here being limited, we commenced making acquaintance with the objects of interest appertaining to the place, and of these the first chosen was the scene of the battle, of course—the gallant attack and final capture of the citadel by General Wolfe. The "Heights of Abraham" is a singular appellation, but I can find no means of enlightenment here as to the origin of the name. There is a fine monument erected on the spot where Wolfe fell (almost in the moment of victory), but it is sadly defaced by the relic-hunting people who have come here at different times, and who have actually hewn off bits of the stone of which it is composed in some of the most prominent places. From Cape Diamond, the promontory on which the citadel is built, the view is magnificent. The St. Lawrence is seen winding its silvery way

through forests and through ravines till it gradually
fades in the distance, while close beneath us, ships of
all nations, some in movement, some riding at anchor,
give life and cheerfulness to the scene. On leaving
the heights to descend to the lower world, we entered
a garden attached to the Government house. This was
once private, but is now given up to the public as a
sort of pleasure ground. There stands in this garden
a fine pillar, erected to the memory of the two rival
commanders of the English and French armies during the memorable siege. Singularly enough, they
were both mortally struck almost at the same moment,
although Montcalm survived a few hours. The
monument bears an inscription—short, yet eloquent,
consisting only of the two names : — " Wolfe,"
" Montcalm," on either side. On quitting the garden, the custode presented us with two very handsome bouquets which he had gathered for us while
we were moralising over the memento to the rival
heroes. Quebec, the old part of it at least, is most
irregularly built; the houses sometimes, when seen
from a little distance, give the idea of being piled one
upon the top of another; but this very peculiarity
renders it far more picturesque than the newer and
more irreproachably precise towns we have travelled
through in the States. There are two cathedrals,
one Protestant, the other Catholic, and no end of
nunneries and sisterhoods of various denominations.

In the chapel of the Ursuline convent Montcalm is buried; on his tomb is the following inscription: " Honneur à Montcalm.   Le destin en lui dérobant la victoire l'a récompensé par une mort glorieuse." After visiting severally the above-mentioned places, we engaged a carriage for the purpose of taking us to the Falls of Montmorency, which we reached after a drive of eight miles through very fine scenery.   I was both astonished and delighted with this waterfall, all the more so, perhaps, that I had heard nothing about it beforehand.   Were it not heresy to confess such an opinion, I am not sure that I do not admire this as much as Niagara.   There is not, indeed, such an immense body of falling water; but then the height is twice as great, and the surrounding scenery is far more wild and romantic.   Byron's description of the " Hell of Waters " is thoroughly realised here.   The falls are encircled by huge black rocks, and beyond them nothing but the wide expanse of the river.

5th.—This morning was ushered in by a frost, and altogether a bitterly cold day,—quite time to get back to the tropics, I think.   We went after break-fast to see the great stronghold of Quebec, the Cita-del, but with the exception of some " lovely soldiers " as —— used to call them, and a tame bear belonging to one of the regiments, there was nothing to detain or attract unprofessional, that is, non-military visitors; besides, we were nearly blown away by a piercing east wind.   We purpose leaving here this evening *en route* to the South, so I shall probably post this previous to our departure.   Quebec, Montreal, indeed I may say, Canada generally, has pleased me much. The people are so gentle, civil, and above all, so polished in manner.   They combine a good deal of the *old French* school of thorough politeness with our natural characteristic of frankness, *without* rudeness.   Few amalgamations can, I think, be more really allied to perfection than this, and I regret leaving it as much as it is possible (for me, at least) to regret leaving a cold severe climate for a more genial atmosphere. . . . . . In consequence of a slight accident which occurred to some part of the steamer's machinery, a delay of some hours has ensued.   We shall soon be off now, however, so I will close my letter. This night's journey will only be retracing our steps as far as Montreal.

Ever your affectionate,

C.

CHAPTER XII.

Albany, September 7th. — You will see by the date of this, my dear father, that we are now considerably advanced on our return journey to New York, hoping to reach there without misadventure this evening. We landed at Montreal yesterday morning, but were unfortunately too late for the fast train; our progress therefore was tedious and fatiguing. The first portion, notwithstanding, was not unpleasant, as we had plenty of time to see the different places through which we passed, and also to admire the scenery of Lake Champlain, on the margin of which our route lay for some considerable distance, till we reached a town called Burlington, a busy thriving place, and apparently a central point of communication by land and water to all parts. We observed several fine steamers as well as other vessels. Had the weather been warmer it would doubtless have been a pleasanter mode of travelling to have descended the lake by boat instead of " car; " but it is far too cold for aquatic excursions in these

northern parts.   The same reason will prevent our
going down the Hudson, which, as I said, had been
our previous plan.   Soon after leaving Burlington,
the night began to close in upon us, and the most
disagreeable part of the journey ensued.   About
two o'clock this morning we arrived at a village
rejoicing in the name of Rutland, and which will
long remain most unfavourably fixed in our memory
by the privations we had to endure.   It should
appear, that Rutland is one of the places subject to
the operation of the " Maine Liquor Law;" and you
may judge how comfortable it was to be informed
that the only refreshment we could obtain, hungry,
cold, and weary as we were, was their horrid iced
water! wine not being permitted to enter the State
(Vermont I believe it was); and the fires being all
out, we could not get a cup of tea or coffee!   In
this hospitable region we were condemned to remain
for upwards of two hours, getting colder and colder
with the approach of dawn!   At length, as all
things must have an end, we made a fresh start;
and in course of time stopped at Saratoga, where I
must do people the justice to say an excellent breakfast was provided, though I was half afraid, after the
experience of the past night, that we might only
be offered some of the mineral waters for which
Saratoga is celebrated.   This watering-place is the
Baden-Baden of America.   All the *grand monde*

flock here in the season; some to drink the waters, some to dress, some to flirt. In short, the nature of these spas seems to be morally the same all the world over. Saratoga, or rather " The Springs," which is the more common appellation, being now deserted for this season, most of the hotels, boarding-houses, &c., are closed until next summer. The next station of importance we came to bore the classic name of Troy, but as we only remained a few minutes I cannot tell whether it deserves so high-sounding a one; still less whether there are any grounds for bestowing the respective titles of Mount Olympus and Mount Ida, on two pieces of high ground, scarcely hills, situated on the northern and southern environs of the town. A short run of only seven miles brought us here, the prettiest spot (barring New York) I have yet seen in the States, built on the side of a hill bathed by the river Hudson. Albany offers a most commanding appearance. The various public buildings, too, are constructed and placed with equally good judgment and good taste. Of these the most conspicuous is the City Hall, almost in the centre of the town, the dome of which is gilt, consequently a passing sunbeam falling on it renders it visible at a great distance. I am sorry our time will not allow us more than this superficial view, as we doubtless might find much that would interest on a closer examination. Albany received its name

from our James the Second, when Duke of York
and Albany, to whom a grant of the New York
territory was made by his brother Charles after his
successful contest with the Dutch in 1664. . . .

We are now once more at New York, having re-
sumed our journey from Albany half an hour after
the above lines were written. Nothing of moment
occurred on the road until we were within a couple
of miles of our destination, when we had the mis-
fortune to run against a horse attached to a cart
imprudently left too near the line of rails. The
poor animal was killed on the spot, fortunately,
in a moment, but it was a shocking sight to witness.
. . . . I regret very much to find that we must
relinquish our intended visit to New Orleans and the
Mississippi. This is a great disappointment. I had
planned it all so well, and was anticipating a most
agreeable expedition, purposely reserved till the last,
as, from all I have heard, it is the best worth visiting
of all the wonders of the United States. But *l'homme
propose et Dieu dispose.* The yellow fever is raging
there with such intensity that it would be wicked-
ness as well as folly to make the attempt. The
latest accounts are most terrible. The devastation
has been so great and so general as to give the town
the appearance of a city of the dead. Trade and
commerce, even, have almost ceased temporarily. As
this may materially alter our future movements, I

shall bring this letter to a sudden close and despatch
it by to-morrow's mail; but you may expect to
hear very shortly again, informing you of whatever
fresh projects we may indulge in.   Meanwhile I am
ever your affectionate,

C.

CHAPTER XIII.

New York, September 12*th.* — My dear Father, —
Since returning from our Canadian excursion, we
have been occupied in revisiting the principal objects
of attraction in New York, besides adding some to our
list which had been previously omitted. Strangers here
make a point of going over the splendid hotels, just
as elsewhere one would visit the churches, or in
London the clubs. To these last, the New York
hotels bear indeed the principal resemblance. The
St. Nicholas is, I think, the finest specimen : its
façade of white marble beautifully sculptured, and
the interior very like the Reform Club. In addition
to the public living rooms there are some very
magnificently decorated and furnished " bridal cham-
bers " for the especial benefit of newly married people
who may have the moral courage to go and spend
their honeymoon *en evidence* before all the world.
But I believe the American couples do not make
any objection. The St. Nicholas is no less than

six stories high. There are also the Metropolitan, the New York, the Astor House, and Delmonico's, all hotels more or less celebrated. We found Taylor's, a fine establishment on the principle of the Parisian Restaurants, to be very well worth a visit. The saloon where you dine or sup is scarcely inferior to " Les trois Frères " in magnificence and decoration, though, by a curious singularity of taste, it is sub-terranean. We went with our friends the D.'s the night before last to supper there, and had a most excellent repast. Some of the most appreciated specimens of the New York cuisine were ordered, so that we might know what was considered best. Fish they cook in great perfection; oysters espe-cially, they dress in innumerable ways. Two dishes I remarked as particularly worthy of commendation, were woodcocks stewed with truffles and écrevisses, and ham boiled in champagne. Previously to this supper party we had been to Christy's and heard some new songs. One I must tell you all about; the enthusiastic manner in which it was received, show-ing pretty plainly what Mrs. Beecher Stowe may expect if she returns to her "ain countrie." The song purported to be concerning some one called " Aunt Sarah;" but was evidently directed to her. The first line I could not catch, but apostrophising Aunt Sarah it continued thus : —

E

" Go talk against your country !
Put money in your purse !
But when the happy 'Darkie'
You mention in your prayer,
Just don't forget the *white slave*
That's starving over there ! "

I never heard such a cheer in my life as burst forth
at these words; it was positively terrific. I should
not like to be in Mrs. S.'s place if she were to come
back before her country people have time to cool
down. They seem inclined to make her pay rather
dearly for what she has written; but, from all I can
gather at present, the Americans, and especially the
American women, are annoyed that a party of English
women, including members of our aristocracy, should
have (to speak plainly), without knowing what they
were talking about, issued a sort of manifesto containing a number of positive errors in point of fact,
and arguing upon premises and assumptions which
did not exist. So say the people here, at least; for
my part, I know nothing of the matter, *pour ou
contre*, beyond trying, but unsuccessfully, to wade
through " Uncle Tom," by which I obtained as much,
or rather more, information on the subject than I required. . . .   Yesterday we paid a visit to the
Croton Waterworks, a wonderful monument of human
industry. The great reservoir is said to be five miles
long, and is able to contain five million gallons of
water. This being forty miles off we did not see, but

contented ourselves with the more easily attained
portion of the works where the aqueduct crosses the,
Harlem River, at a distance of about eight miles.
This spot is called the High Bridge, and well merits
the slight trouble of the excursion. The view is fine,
I should think, under all circumstances, but especially now that the trees are beginning to wear their
autumnal tints; the hues are so dazzling, so rich, so
varied, that I must renounce, as hopeless, any effort
at description, for I am sure you would accuse me of
exaggeration. For my own part, were I to see, or
rather to have seen, such colours transferred to canvass, I should have unhesitatingly exclaimed, " That is
unnatural ! " I must not forget to notice in this chronicle of things new and strange the steam ferry-boats
which we have now used on several occasions, in the
course of our excursions to the various environs of the
city: viz., New Jersey, Brooklyn, Staten Island, &c.
Their appearance is that of a little floating town.
Seen at a short distance, one might fancy a block of
houses had detached itself from the remainder of the
street, and gone for an aquatic promenade, accompanied by all the men, women, children, horses, carriages, carts, pigs, dogs, baskets, and wheelbarrows it
could find on the way. A voyage in one of these
monster conveyances is one of the most amusing
incidents in the New York life, at least to a stranger.
We have paid several visits to the Great Exhibition

E 2

which has been opened here in imitation of the London building. This too is chiefly of glass. It is in a circular form, but much smaller and every way inferior to ours. It is, however, a very good bazaar, but that is all; moreover, I am informed it is a mere private speculation, and that, consequently, the President was rather embarrassed at finding Lord Ellesmere was sent on behalf of our Queen.

This is our last day at New York. We are to sail to-morrow, bound for Mexico, as the few hurried lines I last wrote will have informed you; I will have a letter all prepared to despatch from Havana, giving you the latest intelligence. Till then adieu.

Your ever affectionate,

C.

CHAPTER XIV.

New York (*Astor House*), *September* 16*th.*— My dear Father,—Behold us here still, in spite of all our anticipations to the contrary. A most untoward accident has occurred. We proceeded, according to arrangement, on the morning of the 13th, to the quay of embarkation, having taken our berths in the Crescent City, bound for Havana. On reaching the pier with our luggage and all prepared for the voyage, we were very coolly told that the Crescent City had taken her departure for California the night before! It appears that the Georgia (another of the same Company's vessels), which had started for California some days previously, broke down when off Cape Hatteras; the Crescent City being the only other boat ready, she was sent to the assistance of the Georgia and her passengers, and we poor unfortunate mortals were *plantés là.* After a long delay and an immense deal of talking, they at last promised to forward us by another boat called the George Law, though not before this (the 16th), and at night, for the very unsatis-

factory reason that this vessel, the George Law, is
not yet quite finished!   All this is exceedingly
vexatious, for, among other consequences, this delay
may make us too late for the English steamer due at
Havana on the 24th, in which event farewell to our
contemplated trip to Mexico.

7 o'clock, P.M.—We are off at last. .   .   .   .   .   .

CHAPTER XV.

Vera Cruz, September 28th.— At length we have
safely passed the dangers and overcome the delays of
our voyage, and have landed here all well this morning.   Nearly the whole of the first part of our progress after leaving New York consisted, however, of
a series of disasters and discomforts ; and although we
fortunately reached Havana in time to catch the Mexican mail, we nevertheless took eight days in accom-
plishing what is usually done in four, namely, the
passage between the two ports.

As I before mentioned, the vessel was in a very
unfinished condition, and among the minor evils we
had to endure was the sticking to everything we
touched, the paint and varnish being quite fresh :
then in the hurry of departure they had forgotten to
provide lamps to light either the saloon or cabins, so
at sunset we were obliged to turn into our berths,
until the weather getting warmer as we approached
Havana enabled us to stay on deck at night.   Last
and worst of all, when we had been at sea barely

E 4

two days we were alarmed in the middle of the night by the vessel suddenly coming to a dead stop. Soon one passenger after another stole up to inquire what had happened, but did not come down again; so, to end this state of suspense, I dressed myself as well as I could in the dark and went on deck. All the information I could get from the captain, who was in a shockingly bad humour, was that something, I forget what, had burst, but there was no danger, " if the weather kept calm." This was anything but pleasant intelligence ; luckily, however, the calm continued, and with our disabled engine we reached Havana at length, as I have said, in seven days more. Since the accident we proceeded, I am informed, at the rate of three knots an hour only. We had no sails either, that part of the " fixings," like many others, not being completed. But from Havana I am glad to say all has gone prosperously. A sunny sky and a calm sea. We passed in safety the famous " Alacranes," Anglice " Scorpions," a dangerous reef of rocks so called ; the terror of all sea-going people in these parts. Besides the ordinary danger of being driven upon them in stormy weather, there is the additional peril of a current so strong as to render it excessively difficult, under the most favourable circumstances, to keep a correct "reckoning," as I believe it is nautically termed, consequently many have been the ships drawn to their destruction. Even steamers do not

escape sometimes: within the last ten years, two of
the West India packets have been wrecked on the
Alacranes.   Before casting anchor in the bay of Vera
Cruz we passed the famous castle and fortress of St.
Jean d'Ulloa.   It seems much the worse for the siege
by the Prince de Joinville in 1838.   The country has
been also in too disturbed a state, apparently, to
allow of reparations being made.   Landed at nine
o'clock, and in consequence of the English consul
having written a very civil note, putting himself and
all he possessed at my disposition, we went at once to
his house and were received most cordially.   Found
a large budget of letters from England awaiting us,
and after having perused them and made necessary
inquiries concerning the ways and means of journey-
ing to Mexico from here, we went to the Hotel de las
Diligencias, where we shall remain until to-morrow
afternoon.   I am rather agreeably surprised with
the general appearance of Vera Cruz, having heard it
described as a "hole;" in short, as everything that was
bad, whereas I find it anything but dirty, and tolerably wide streets, and by no means offensive looking,
rather the contrary. It has a look of antiquity, and, to a
certain degree, of sadness, but that rather adds to the
interest of its aspect.   The first peculiarity I observed
was a crowd of vultures, called here "Sopilotes."
They hover about in all directions, looking for prey,
anything dead which may fall in their way.   They

E 5

are melancholy looking creatures, but quite tame.
Apropos of beasts of prey; just before landing to-day,
we amused ourselves in watching the manœuvres of
a shark who kept swimming all round us, apparently
in the hope of catching something good for his breakfast.   I fear he was disappointed in his expectations,
as, with the exception of a small piece of dry bread
which the cook had thrown at him, there was nothing
to satisfy his craving.   At three o'clock we dined and
had our first experience of Mexican cookery.   The
dishes are rather strongly seasoned with chilis, pep-
pers, &c., but no doubt, when once accustomed to the
cuisine I shall find it by no means bad.   The sauces
are excellent, and very scientifically mixed.   Took a
walk this evening with the young son of the English
consul, who good-naturedly volunteered to be our
cicerone. We directed our steps first to the Alameda,
a name given generally to the public promenades in
Mexico.   The scene here was very pretty, and with
the adjuncts of a setting sun, a clear bright sky, and
an old ruined castle, was almost romantic. To-morrow
we start on our adventurous journey. I wonder what
will become of us between this and Mexico. We hear
wonderful tales of robbery, but we must hope for the
best.   So now farewell for the present.

Your ever affectionate,

C.

CHAPTER XVI.

Jalapa, September 30th.-- My dear Father,— We arrived here at 5 o'clock this afternoon, nine hours after our time; but the wonder seems to me that we are here at all. Such roads! or rather such a want of them. The old adage came to my recollection, " If you'd seen these roads before they were made," &c. But we *have* seen these. It is perfectly incomprehensible to me how any carriages built by mortal hands could bear even one of the fearful knocks, or rather I should say, *leaps,* of which we have been suffering a succession to-day and last night. We had generally eight horses or mules drawing us, and I do not think I am exaggerating when I say that, during the nineteen hours we have been on the road, we have not passed over 100 yards of level ground; stones, holes, rocks, sand-banks, chasms both wide and deep—over all of which we made a succession of leaps. In short, I am almost too much bruised and shaken to describe our progress: if this continues, I don't think we shall have a whole bone left in our

bodies.   To mend matters, we had to get out of the
diligence two or three times in the middle of the
night, and walk some distance through the mud and
in the dark, so as to lighten the conveyance sufficiently to enable it to take a kind of flying leap over
some unusually wide chasm in the road.   Apart from
these grievances, however, and when we could manage
to keep ourselves still for a few minutes at a time,
and look around us, the scenery was most lovely,
and the approach to Jalapa will never be effaced from
my recollection.   How nature has showered every
beauty and every blessing on this land! I have read
in fairy tales, and in descriptions of what Paradise
was supposed to be, of scenes something like this;
but that such places really existed on the earth
I could not have believed unless I had come here.

October 1st.—We slept last night at Jalapa, being
far too much tired to attempt continuing our route,
so shall wait and take our chance of finding vacant
places in the carriage to-day.   Received a visit from
Mr. Kennedy, an English gentleman living here, and
to whom I had a letter of introduction, and who is
to show us all the beauties of Jalapa if we should
not leave this afternoon.   Meanwhile, as I was writing the above, I was interrupted by the diligence
dashing or rather leaping up to the door, and finding
that there were two vacant places we were soon again
en route.   As we advanced, the scenery was, if possi-

ble, even more enchanting than on the other side of
Jalapa. The most distinguishing feature, at least, so
it appears to me, is the profusion—the wilderness of
flowers spread on every side. The ground is literally
enamelled with them, and every tree and shrub
loaded with the most beautiful and brilliant hued
parasites clinging and creeping to the topmost boughs
of even the highest trees. So dazzling an array of
colours I never saw grouped together— crimson, scarlet, blue, orange, purple, of all forms and sizes, and
last, though not least in loveliness, the pure white
blossoms of the datura, the most ordinary of wild
flowers here, and named "El Floripundio." The
snowy peak of Orizava, which we had constantly in
sight yesterday, was now hidden from our view. I
believe the next mountain of importance we shall
make acquaintance with will be the Cofre de Perote,
about half way between Vera Cruz and Mexico.

October 4th, Hotel San Augustin, Mexico. —We
reached here yesterday at 4 P.M., after several hair-
breadth escapes and adventures which I shall now
try to record ; but the constant travelling and excessive fatigue quite prevented me writing daily since
quitting Jalapa. On that same night, the 1st October, got to Perote about 11 o'clock, a dismal-looking
place, and where we had to sleep almost in a stable
yard—that is, our bed-room was only separated by
means of a glass door from the various denizens of

the stable and farm. The sleeping, however, was but nominal, as we were aroused again at three in the morning, and tired, cold, and exhausted, with sleepy companions and a lowering sky we set forth on our night march. The only satisfactory reflexion we enjoyed being, that we were provided with an armed escort; as soon as daylight appeared, however, they left us.

CHAPTER XVII.

October 2*nd.*—This day's journey was very tedious and
wearying, an almost constant ascent. The air becoming colder and colder, the country arid and sandy.
The flowers had left us, and in their stead there was
little to be seen save some dwarf pines and patches
of brushwood here and there, but all the rest a sandy
waste.   Above all loomed the black and gloomy
Cofre de Perote, so named from the summit of the
mountain being shaped like a box or chest, for which
"Cofre" is the Spanish word.   Towards the end of
the day, however, matters began again to improve,
and I have no doubt, if we had been able to distinguish the scenery, we should have been better pleased;
but it was seven o'clock when we reached Puebla, and
very nearly dark.   There we enjoyed a refreshing
night's rest, preceded by an excellent supper.   We
were offered, among other dishes, some very nice
preserve, called Cabella de Angel, or Angel's hair,
a fanciful and pretty name.   It has the appearance
of long golden threads, and tastes like crystallised

sugar. I could not make out of what it was made. At a little village on our road to day, we had for the first time some pulque, the national and favourite drink of the Mexicans. It is most abominable both in scent and taste; yet it is said, that although the first impression with every one is the same, that nevertheless in a very short time you not only get accustomed to it, but become most inordinately fond of it. This may be so, but I do not think we shall be long enough in Mexico to acquire the taste. "Pulque" is made, I believe, from the flower of the maguey plant, a sort of large aloe, which grows in profusion all over the country. Hedges and fences are here made by nature, both of the maguey and the prickly pear. The latter is generally called by its Indian name, "Nopal," and is used as the national emblem on the coins, like our rose, thistle, and shamrock. We must hope for an opportunity of seeing Puebla on our return, as this time, having arrived after dark and started before four in the morning, we were unable to judge of its appearance. In point of size and population it is the next to Mexico. Yesterday, though the last day of our journey hither, was the most fertile in adventure. First of all, we had to pass through the "robbers' tract" of country, and were for some hours in momentary expectation of being attacked. The spot chosen by these heroes for their depredations is singularly well adapted for

the purpose; a dark thick wood concealing two deep
ravines on either side, rocks and caves in all directions, afford excellent ground for ambuscade and
sudden attacks on the unwary. This part of the
country is very appropriately named the " Black
Hole." We were fortunately, however, *quittes
pour la peur*, and saw no living robber. But about
three miles after leaving Rio Frio, a small village
.where we had stopped to breakfast, we were horrified
at passing, within a distance of half a yard, the body
of a man hung to the branches of a tree by a cord
passed round his waist. The upper part of his
body was naked and much stained with blood, apparently recently shed. It was a shocking spectacle, but what his history was we had yet to learn.
On reaching Mexico in the evening, we heard
to our consternation that the diligence, which
left Vera Cruz the day before us (and in which I was
rather vexed at not being able to secure places), had
been robbed on the road, and everything taken from
the passengers. A young man, Mr. Buchanan, one
of our fellow voyagers in the Avon to Vera Cruz,
begged the bandits to let him keep his desk, after
they should have convinced themselves that it contained nothing but private papers of his own,
and of no use to any one else. The man of whom
he asked this favour consented, and was about to
give him back his desk, when one of the robbers

demurred, and insisted on taking it. It was this
very man who was shot, and whose body we saw
hanging to the tree. It appeared that the diligence, having met a party of soldiers soon after their
attack, told them what had occurred, and on which
they had immediately proceeded to the scene of
action. Before long they overtook the gang, shot
one dead, as it happened, he who had the desk in
his hands, and wounded two of the others. They
hung up the dead man at once to a tree, as a
warning. All robbers now caught are instantly
shot without trial, and their bodies hung up *in
terrorem* as a warning to others. This is Santa
Anna's last edict. A dreadfully severe one, certainly,
and yet it seems impossible to remedy the evil.
The constant revolutions and changes of government
in this distracted country have the effect of rendering the law a dead letter. To turn from this
unpleasant theme, I must note down some observa-
tions on the world-famed valley of Mexico, as the
view of it bursts, or ought to burst, on the sight on
attaining the "heights" about forty miles from the
city. After traversing many miles of unceasing toil,
jumps, jolts, and leaps, we at length gained the long-
wished for eminence whence Mexico in all her glory
should have shown herself to our longing gaze. But,
alas for mortal expectations! the clouds had collected deeply and thickly, and of the splendid pano-

rama we had anticipated scarcely two-thirds were visible. The two snow-crowned volcanoes, Popocatepetl and Iztaccihuatl, were completely shrouded in mist; so that altogether we must class the " view " as *a dream*, to come true in the future I hope. To-day we have done nothing beyond " fixing " ourselves, as the Yankees say,—installed ourselves comfortably in our rooms, unpacked our things, and received a visit from our Minister, Mr. Doyle; after which we occupied ourselves till dusk in looking out of the window, here a very edifying employment, when every human being that passes is a picture in him or herself. We took a short walk this evening in the Plaza. The people most do congregrate in a part of it called *las Cadenas,* from the chains linking together the rails in front of the cathedral. I shall now conclude this long letter, hoping it may reach its destination safely.

Ever your affectionate,

C.

CHAPTER XVIII.

Mexico, Hotel San Augustin, October 9th.—My
dear Father, ... I hope this will be an acceptable
present to you, being the only birth-day memorial
circumstances at this moment allow of my sending.
We found full occupation the first morning or two
after our arrival in making topographical discoveries,
and tracing out a few plans of our future movements.
In the former there is not much difficulty, for the
streets are large, wide, and run chiefly at right angles
from one another.   It is a very beautiful town, judging of it even by its external appearance only : it may
well be called a city of palaces, for I do not recollect
observing a single poor or mean-looking house in it.
The extreme clearness of the atmosphere causes even
the far-distant mountains to appear close at the end
of the vista formed in every street; yet the nearest
mountain is forty miles off. . . . . When *chez moi* I
find the attraction of the balcony almost irresistible.
The men with their graceful " serapes," and the
women with their *un*graceful " rebosos "— the dark

eyes and swarthy complexions common to both sexes;
then add to these the singular, and, in some instances,
musical cries of the various vendors of goods, eata-
bles, and drinkables, and you have a scene quite
unsurpassable in its way. The varieties of complexion are curious; every shade from pale yellow to
dark copper colour is to be found here. The "serape"
is a kind of double blanket of the most brilliant and
varied hues : a hole in the centre admits the head of
the wearer, and the two ends may be worn either
simply hanging down from the neck, before and
behind, or may be twisted round the body, or thrown
mantilla-fashion over the shoulders. Among other
natural curiosities I saw an Indian chief going to sell
some embroidered things at market. He was dressed
in a tunic of fur, and wore a beautiful crown of
ostrich feathers on his head. I do not think the
Mexican people have good expressions, though their
features are generally handsome; but they have a
downward look about the eyes which is unpleasant,
and gives one the idea of their having some mischief
always lurking somewhere. They are a strange people from all accounts : they would think nothing of
murdering you, with or without reason; yet they are
as civil, as kind, as ready to oblige, as warm in manner, and as anxious to please, as if your pleasure was
their only care, and that not only to strangers but to
each other. It is difficult to reconcile this apparent

warm-heartedness with the cruel and blood-thirsty natures they show sometimes.

We rode on horseback yesterday morning to Chapultepec, accompanied by Mr. Berkeley and Mr. Portman, the two *attachés*. A most beautiful ride, and affording a far finer view of Mexico than from the Vera Cruz side. This grand old place, so much associated with some of the most stirring events connected with the Mexican Conquest and the history of the days of Cortez and Montezuma, must look very different now from what was its aspect then: so different, indeed, that, could any of the actors in those scenes now rise from their graves and look upon it, I should doubt their being able to recognise, in the stately but sad Chapultepec of the present day, the bright and flowery gardens of which we read so charming a description in the glowing pages of Prescott. Here is to be seen one of the few exceptions to the rule of the unchangeableness of nature. Scarcely three hundred years have elapsed, yet what is now covered with corn-fields, potatoes, *tobacco*, and other necessaries of life to the modern Mexican, was then a vast lake, reflecting on its glassy surface the cypress trees and pleasure gardens of this favourite resort of Montezuma. The aqueduct, too, now broken and in ruins, like those on the old Roman Campagna, then conveyed its pure and bountiful supplies to all the thirsty city. On the other hand, the most striking feature now offered to the eye is the magnificent castle or stronghold, built on the summit of the porphyry rock, once the burial place of the Indian kings. One of the Spanish vice-kings, named Galvez, was the projector and builder of this fortress, towards the end of the last century. His avowed purpose was simply the erection of a summer residence for his own pleasure, but as the work of construction advanced it assumed so greatly the form of a fortification, which in such a neighbourhood was considered by the Government at home, and not unreasonably, I think, as too regal an abode for a subject, and consequently it was *annexed* by the Crown, though unlike some other annexations I have heard of, Galvez, the original owner, was well compensated for his outlay. But the building was never furnished internally, having, even in its present state, says Madame Calderon de la Barca, cost the Spanish 300,000 dollars. The general appearance, shape, and situation of the Castle of Chapultepec reminds me very much (its colour only excepted) of the old German fortress of Heidelberg. The rocky and wooded hill, the river and the valley, with the fertile plain spread beyond, mark both. Further the parallel cannot be drawn, as from Heidelberg no splendid imperial city can be seen. It would be difficult indeed to find one in Europe now that could compare in grandeur with Mexico. Rome or Athens

in former days might have done so, but in their
present state can scarcely even rival her in architecture (barring always St. Peter's, which stands alone
" of temples old or altars new"). The present Re-
publican Government have turned the old Castle into
a college, for teaching young military ideas how to
shoot. Entirely surrounding the sides and base of
the hill on which the Castle is built are the most
gigantic cypress trees that I imagine exist in the
·world; their appearance is altogether so extraordinary, that when once they have arrested the attention
it is difficult either to look at or think of anything
else. It is certain from the ancient chronicles and
accounts that have been handed down to us, that
these trees were not only living but had attained
their full growth at the time of Cortez's invasion and
conquest. One of these, called *par excellence* Montezuma's, is of the immense circumference of fifty feet.
They all now wear a most curious appearance; a
kind of parasite, or moss of a greyish white colour,
twines about their trunks, and hangs in wild profusion from their branches. It has the exact appearance of long grey hair, and, especially being con-
trasted with the deep almost black colour of the
cypress branches, has a most singular effect. The
local names given to these hairy-looking masses are
" Bisnagas " or " Cabeza de·Viejo " (old man's head).

MEXICO FROM TACUBAYA.

The cypress trees themselves are called "Ahuahuetes." After wandering about for some time in the "cold shade" of this forest "aristocracy," we remounted our steeds and went to Tacubaya, which formed a kind of suburb of Mexico, and is a good deal frequented by the residents there when they wish to change air or scene. There are several pretty villas, with gardens attached, studded about. In one of these we were very hospitably entertained at breakfast; our host was an Englishman, Mr. Geaves, with a pretty wife and sister-in-law, both much admired in this country, where the fair and bright English complexion is as rare as beautiful. Tacubaya would almost appear to be one vast flower garden; the profusion of roses of all hues and sizes is really astonishing. Among other notable personages who are ruralising here at present is General Santa Anna, the actual President of the Mexican Republic, consequently, one constantly meets or is overtaken by aide-de-camps, messengers, soldiers, &c., riding in hot haste to and fro; some of them, too, looking so big with importance that they might have been bearers, at least, of tidings of some new *pronunciamento*. Before returning home we went to the top of Mr. Geaves's house, called the "Azotea," to look at the surrounding view, which is the same as from Chapultepec, but with the very important addition of that fine old castle and its grey-bearded trees, which

F

it need scarcely be said are no inconsiderable features in the general beauty of the landscape.

I find I have forgotten to mention that the day before yesterday we dined at the Embassy with Mr. Doyle, and afterwards accompanied him to the opera, called (till further orders) El Teatro de Santa Anna. It is a good-sized house, and handsomely though heavily decorated; but it is far inferior in every way to the Tacon at Havana. The performers, on the other hand, seem better; the voices excellent; and for the most part both men and women seem to be thorough musicians. It would be difficult to pronounce upon their personal appearance, however, for the theatre is so badly lighted that one person can scarcely be distinguished from another.

We rode this morning to the Paseo before breakfast. Notwithstanding the early hour, all the world was abroad in carriages or on horseback. The former are lumbering awkward looking machines, something like German coaches. Singularly enough, they do not seem here to have a notion of the pleasure or convenience of an open carriage; the more inexplicable an omission in a climate so peculiarly adapted for such an enjoyment. It seemed to me quite a waste of the bounties of nature, with a warm but not hot sun shining, a soft and balmy air, to see half a dozen people caged up in one of these ponderous vehicles, one head peeping above another at the nar-

row window. This can scarcely be called taking an
airing. Nothing can be more picturesque, on the
other hand, than the Mexican cavalier's costume,
when adhered to in its true character, and not "improved," or "spoilt" (the terms in this case being
synonymous), by the introduction of English or
Yankee fashions. The dress has been so often described and is so familiar to most people, that it
would seem almost a work of supererogation to give
a catalogue *raisonnée* of its component parts. The
Paseo we visited this morning is called "El Paseo de
Bucarelli," the viceroy of that name having planned
it, and during whose government it was completed.
It bears the same family resemblance to all other
Paseos, Alamedas, and public promenades I have
already mentioned elsewhere. The different species
of trees growing along their sides being the chief
points by which one may distinguish the public
walks of one country or town from another: thus, at
Havana the palm tree is the chosen one; here it is
the pepper tree, a native of Peru, I believe, originally;
it takes, nevertheless, kindly to this soil, and though
not possessing the grandeur or majestic bearing of
the palm, is still excessively graceful and beautiful
in its own way. The leaves are of a dark shining
green, and the fruit or pepper berries bright scarlet.
They grow in bunches, not unlike the mountain ash in
size and colour; but instead of forming one large head

of berries like it, the pepper grows like bunches of grapes, hanging downwards like them, or *deciduously* as perhaps you would say.

E. has gone with the Legation to a bull fight; but that being an exhibition I have never been able to make up my mind to witness (*unless* I could make sure of seeing some of the men killed who so cruelly torture the bulls, and, far worse still, their helpless and courageous horses), I have profited by the opportunity of enjoying a tranquil hour or two in writing to you.

Ever yours affectionately,

C.

CHAPTER XIX.

Mexico, October 12*th.*—This morning, my dear
Father, we devoted to the Paseo de las Vigas: went
by one road and returned across the fields by another.
Had a splendid view of the whole valley and the chain
of mountains in all their glory, including the two
volcanoes, Popocatepetl and Iztaccihuatl; the English for the latter name is " The White Lady." Some
say it was called after the beautiful Indian mistress
of Cortez, Malintzin, the Malinche hills being the
group of which Iztaccihuatl is the chief. Malintzin
was christened soon after the Spaniards had entered
Mexico, being named Marina, and it was as Doña
Marina she played so important and romantic a part
in the history of the conquest. It is a wondrous love
tale, and far outstrips in its unadorned veracity the
imaginations of most writers of fiction. The affection,
so sudden in its growth, yet so faithful and so true,
through good report and through evil, remained un-
changing to the end, at least to *her* end,—that is, when
she was married, literally disposed of,—when the news

came that the legitimate wife of Cortez was leaving
Spain to join him in the new world. I have often
speculated on what Doña Marina's thoughts and
feelings may have been on this subject. Did she
know of the tie which bound her lover, or was that
tenet of the Christian faith which binds husband
and wife to each other only till death, left un-
taught to her, when she threw her lot with Cortez,
and made his God her God? And then when the
last and worst trial came for both,— when the almost
hated but still lawful wife of Cortez appeared on the
scene, did Marina yield to persuasion, entreaty,
threats, in consenting to marry another, or was it an
expiation? Did she hope to "bear the martyr's
cross, to win the martyr's crown?" *Quien sabe!*
But it's a strange tale, and would make a fertile
theme for the romance writer. The name of Doña
Marina's husband was Don Juan de Jamarillo.   It is
rarely found, in other cases bearing any resemblance
to this, that the name of the second hero should be
rescued from oblivion; but this certainly, it must be
owned, was an exceptional circumstance. It is very
provoking, however, that from the time of her
marriage no further record of her life is to be met
with, not even of the period or manner of her death.
Whether she was happy, or miserable, or neither,
but "contented," tradition sayeth not: only the
kindly feeling and grateful recollection with which

even to this day her name is mentioned as the good
angel both of Spain and Mexico in those stormy
times.   To return to our promenade after this flight
of imagination; the *Paseo de las Vigas* is frequented during part of the year (the spring and
early summer from March till May, I believe) as the
fashionable lounge instead of the Buccarelli ; the
chief attraction there, consisting in the drive, being
along the borders of the canal.   While the Mexican
beau monde disport themselves in their carriages, or
on their caracoling horses, the picturesque-looking
Indians with their families are rowing or floating
past on their canoes laden with flowers and fruit.
At all times this must be a pleasing spectacle, and
even now as we witnessed it to-day, though not
"the season," the *coup d'œil* was most attractive.
The Indian love for flowers is almost a religion ;
and the way in which they decorate not merely their
persons, but every object they employ in daily life,
with these natural ornaments, throws a halo of
beauty and romance over the commonest things.
In the spring and flowering time, of course, the
brilliancy of the show is enhanced tenfold; hence
the fashionable season for *las Vigas* occurs at that
period.   I have propounded a theory !   Nothing very
abstruse ; it concerns " only a woman's hair," that
is to say, the way of dressing it ; but it seems to me
that the mode of wearing the hair plaited *en cou-*

ronne round the head, which we have adopted of
late, and the Italians many years ago, must have
been of Indian origin.   How the Europeans obtained it would be another fertile field of argument,
as   difficult perhaps, though less important to determine than the much vexed question, whence
the traces of the symbols of the Christian faith,
which have been found in Mexico to have existed
ages before the existence of America was known?
. . . . To return to the hair.   Every Indian
woman you meet, whatever may be her calling or
occupation, wears her hair in a heavy coil or plait
across the head, and this plait is invariably studded,
either with bright coloured flowers, or (and this is
the more common way) interlaced with what looks
like a crimson cord, but is in reality the long leaf
of an aquatic plant dyed to the colour. Talking of
costume, I took advantage of a short interval of
leisure to-day, to pay a visit to a vendor of wax
figures ; for the manufacture of which the Mexicans
are so famous. You would most likely remember
seeing some beautiful specimens at the Great Exhibition.   We have made several purchases, as
presents for home friends, though I greatly fear
they will get broken in the course of the long
journey they will have to take. One of the women
I bought represents a fruit seller, and it is really
wonderful to observe the minuteness with which every

single article in her basket is copied from nature.
The same with her dress; every stripe, every thread
in the various garments she wears, is to the life.
My man is a pulque seller, with the sort of pipe or
cask containing the delicious beverage on his back.
He wears a magnificent *serapé*, silver earrings,
pointed hat, and the orthodox double pair of un-
mentionables, ornamented down each " limb " with a
row of silver buttons.   Adieu, now, *hasta luego*.   I
am getting on pretty well in Spanish.

Ever your affectionate,

C.

CHAPTER XX.

Mexico, October 14*th.*—Yesterday, my dear Father, we had a most busy day,— a regular round of sight-seeing. First of all, we had a diplomatic riding-party, Spain, France, and England contributing a representative. Thus escorted, we set off at the early hour of seven in the morning on a pilgrimage to the shrine of Nuestra Señora de Guadeloupe, about four miles distant. This Virgin is the person who does everything needful for Mexico and the Mexicans; consequently she is held in great esteem, and many are the offerings dedicated to her. We went into the church, but did not linger there very long, as there is not much now in it to attract or interest strangers. Formerly the altar and railing were of solid silver; but now that is all changed. The real ore has been melted down, and in its stead there is now but a tawdry *tin*-looking imitation. The miraculous picture, which, as the legend relates, was painted in one night by the Mater Dolorosa herself on the cloak of an Indian who had fallen asleep enshrouded in its folds, we looked at as in duty bound. This picture, in any time of trouble or need, is carried about in public from church to church, by way of reminding the heavenly artist of the protection she volunteered in former days to Mexico. The principal object of our expedition, however, was the view from another chapel on the top of a steepish hill, also dedicated to the Virgin. Here we were amply repaid for our early rising; everything was literally *couleur de rose*, bathed in the beautiful early sunlight, the air soft and laden with perfume. There is here close to the chapel a most extraordinary structure, erected by a Spaniard as an *ex voto* offering to the Lady of Guedaloupe for having delivered him from the perils of shipwreck. It is made of brick, or something that looks like brick, and is in the shape and of the size of the mainsail of a ship, — an original notion, at any rate, though the effect is not very happy in the execution. Cantered back to breakfast after this very enjoyable excursion with good spirits and rather extra good appetites. Later in the day we visited the Mint, and saw the whole process of making and coining the dollars. It was most interesting to me, as it happened I had never seen anything of the sort before. The director of the Mint made me a present of a dollar that I had seen go through its various transmutations. On leaving this, we went to the

Mineria, or school of mines. It contains a collection
of mineral productions of various kinds, very much
like all other such assemblages, only not quite so
good as most. But the thing to be seen is the
palace which contains them, not the contents themselves. It is a wonderfully beautiful edifice—I should
imagine on the model of the Alhambra; the Moorish
arches and columns, the fountains and general exu-
berance of ornament, is quite what I suppose the
Alhambra to be. The architect of this Mexican
chef d'œuvre was Tolosa. We next proceeded to the
University, in the court of which there is a very fine
equestrian statue of Charles IV. of Spain. The
statue is of bronze, and is a masterpiece of the same
sculptor; but a statue, however beautiful, is no such
uncommon thing: the singularity of this is, that the
horse is represented trotting in the peculiar manner
the Spanish call *el paso*, and we, I believe, call
ambling; that is, the fore and hind legs of the same
side advancing together. In another part of this
courtyard is preserved that frightful relic of barba-
rism, the sacrificial stone, with the notch cut out in
it for resting the head of the victim while he was
being subjected to tortures which it makes one's
blood curdle to think of. The sacrifice was to pro-
pitiate the gods of the barbarians, who afterwards,
to please themselves, cooked and ate the remains.
I cannot, after reading the accounts which have

been transmitted to us of these horrors, either
pity the Indians or wonder at the Spaniards com-
mitting any cruelties upon the savages when they
had the opportunity; for it must be remembered
that on many occasions when the fortune of war
had delivered some of Cortez's people into the
hands of the Aztecs, they were put to death with
all the same accessories of torment as those sacrificed
to the gods, and in the sight and almost hearing of
their comrades.   We made an ineffectual attempt to
see the Museum, but some reparations are going on
which will keep it closed for another week or so.
We obtained access, however, to the Botanical Garden
which is attached to it.   The state of neglect into
which this has fallen is quite melancholy.   I suppose,
because Providence has allowed everything to grow
without any trouble, the people consequently will
not give themselves any.   We had a gorgeous
bouquet presented to each of us, including flori-
pundios, white and red, besides many other beautiful-
hued flowers of which I do not know the botanical
names and do not understand the Mexican; but I
remarked nevertheless that all these blossoms, lovely
as they undoubtedly were, were of the most ordinary
description in Mexico, every cottage garden, or
rather what would answer to such with us, containing
them all.   I told the gardener I thought he had a
sinecure and employed his time accordingly, at which

he seemed much affronted. Concluded this busy day with a dinner at the Spanish Embassy. The present envoy of Spain to the Mexican Republic is the Marquis de la Ribera. The Captain-General, who is a very old friend of his, gave me a letter of introduction, and we have found both him and Madame de Ribera among the kindest and best of the many friends we have made among the Spanish people. The Marquise is truly, and in the best sense of the word, " a charming woman," uniting the most endearing qualities in herself. She is a daughter of the Duc de Rivas, thereby possessing some of the best blood in Spain.

CHAPTER XXI.

Real del Monte, Oct. 15th, 11 P.M. — We left Mexico at six this morning, on our way to the far-famed silver mines of Real del Monte. We had engaged a diligence to take us the first fifty miles, which chiefly traverse a plain, and had sent on our horses to meet us at the village of Haltepec, together with our escort, twenty-four men (mounted) whom Santa Anna, acceding to the request Mr. Doyle had made in our behalf, kindly granted for our protection against the perils of the route, said to be considerable in these parts. The officer in command of the escort travelled with us in the "waggon." Just as we arrived at Haltepec, a divertissement occurred which thoroughly disturbed my gravity for the rest of the journey. For some time I had been very uncomfortable, owing to the seat of the carriage being so high; my feet could not reach the ground, and, after sundry attempts to obtain some resting-place for them, I did at last touch something under the seat opposite to me; and, finding it yield, I gradually, with the aid of

both feet, drew it under me (apparently it was a
black bag), and for an hour or two enjoyed a considerable increase of comfort.   When within half a mile
of Haltepec, as I have said, I observed " our Captain "
hunting, fumbling, and peering about in all directions.   At last he approached me, and on stooping
and seeing on what I was reposing my feet, shall I
ever forget the ludicrous horror depicted on his
countenance as he ejaculated " Santa Maria Puris-
sima !!"   I burst into a violent fit of laughter,
when, to make matters better, he seized my ankles
with both hands, rudely pushed them to one side,
and *pointed*, for he was past speech, at the black
bundle under me.   Poor man! no wonder he was
terrified; the bag contained a pair of loaded blunder-
busses, and I had cleverly managed to turn the
muzzles upwards, and pointed to myself.   It was a
miracle, certainly, that I escaped; yet, with it all, the
ridiculous has so far outweighed the dangerous, that
I cannot ever think of it for a moment with becoming
seriousness.   We remained about an hour to refresh
ourselves at Haltepec, then mounted our horses, and
set forth a numerous company; but the weather,
which had previously been fine and sunny, suddenly
changed, and we were caught in a terrific storm
of rain, which unfortunately lasted a considerable
time.   We must have had a most imposing appearance as we galloped into the little village of

Pachuca. About thirty people we were in all, and
the escort, at least, not to speak of ourselves, looked
exceedingly picturesque,—the graceful sombreros, the
flowing serapes, and last, not least, the thorough-
bred-looking horses, nearly all of whom in this
country have Arabian blood. We made a grand
entrée into the court-yard of the hacienda, wet and
dripping as we were. Here our staff of soldiers left
us, after receiving our sincere thanks for their safe-
guard; and I bad adieu to my frightened Captain,
who had not recovered from his *attaque de nerfs*, I
believe, when he left us. We now proceeded to
ascend the hill leading to Real del Monte. The
road is somewhat barren, the maguey and the prickly
pear being the only vegetation growing near; but
the distant mountain scenery is wild and beautiful. Before we arrived at our journey's end it became bitterly cold, and the air so rarefied that
breathing was laborious. This, however, is no great
wonder, as Real is 10,000 feet above the level of the
sea. We were by no means sorry to arrive at Mr.
Auld's house, where we were most hospitably welcomed by him and Mrs. Auld. Mr. Auld is the
director of the mines, and, I believe, a shareholder.
They are worked and managed entirely by an English company. Indeed, so completely English is
the place considered, that in Mexico, when your
friends hear that you contemplate a trip to Real del

Monte, they are accustomed to observe, "You are going to England!" Certainly, several of the peculiarities of our manners and customs were visible immediately on our arrival, but were none the less welcome. Perhaps the most agreeable of all, for the first impression, was the sight of a blazing fire in Mrs. Auld's drawing-room. At any rate, I never remember enjoying one so much even in England. I hope you will give me due credit for my determination in sitting up to write to you at this time of night, for I am very tired and sleepy; but as I anticipate being still more so to-morrow, as we are, I hear, to be on horseback all day, I am afraid, were I to delay my daily chronicle till then, I might forget or omit something which, nevertheless, you might like to know. My next letter will most likely not be written till we are back again in Mexico, but I shall jot down a few notes *en attendant.*

Ever your affectionate,

C.

CHAPTER XXII.

Mexico, 21*st.* — We are once more here again, my dear Father, having accomplished our *English* expedition in safety. Altogether the excursion has been most agreeable. As I told you was my intention, I took notes of the various incidents as they occurred, and therefore I will without further apology transcribe them *tale quale.*

16*th.*—Found this morning that our poor horses were completely knocked up, so much so that it is doubtful if they will be fit for work again for many weeks to come, even if they are then. This is most vexatious, as, should they prove unfit for service as long as this, I shall have paid 60*l.* for this excursion alone, as the horses, with their saddles and accoutrements included, cost me this sum. Mr. Auld, however, provided us with steeds from his stable to-day, and we rode to Regla, once the residence of the Counts of Regla, the owners of all these rich mines. The only house now on the estate is a hacienda (equivalent in English to a farmhouse), where, on

receiving the silver out of the mines, they work and
separate it from the earth in which it is hidden, and
by a series of processes which, although I saw, I
should fear making a mistake were I to attempt to-
describe minutely, they finally form it into bars, in
which state it is forwarded to Mexico, either for
coining there or for exportation to other countries
as specie. The natural beauties of Regla are great;
indeed, during the whole of our ride the scenery was
charming. The hacienda is imbedded in a hole, to
use a common but very expressive word; this same
hole being walled by two gigantic chains of rocks
called by the learned basaltic columns. The name
given them here is the " Giant's Causeway." They
are most curious-looking—resemble the barrels of an
organ, and seem much more as if they were made by
art than nature. The house is now inhabited by the
superintendent of the company, a Mr. Bell, and his
wife, from the north of England.

18th.—Rose at four in the morning, and were in our
saddles at half-past five en route to visit a famous
barranca and see from it the sun rise over the
surrounding mountains. These barrancas are like
what in the Alps are called mountain torrents, only
that in this country they are much more formidable
and much larger; they seem to split the hills asunder
in their headlong course. From the spot whence we
gazed on the magnificent view unrolling itself beneath

and around us, we could discern in the distance many
of these wild and terrible-looking chasms. They are
now dried up, but in the rainy season, the fury of the
waters dashing down these rocky channels, and carrying everything away with their irresistible strength,
it is neither safe nor even possible sometimes to
approach them. We returned to Regla to breakfast,
and afterwards took leave of Mr. and Mrs. Bell, and
retraced our steps home, *i. e.* to Real del Monte.
Mr. Auld took us on our way to visit a hacienda,
called San Miguel, also belonging to the Count de
Regla, a most beautiful spot imbedded in trees, with
a fresh clear lake in the midst of them. The whole
scene had an English park-like appearance, the wonderful flowers only excepted, with which we cannot
vie. At the hacienda itself they are employed, as
most of the other occupants in these parts, in working
the silver after it is taken from the mines, adding
the quicksilver, &c., and making in a fit state for
transport.

19*th.*—Took another ride on horseback through
scenery even more magnificent, if possible, than that
of the barranca. We had to descend a very rugged
and slippery path, and when we reached the bottom
we were nearly swamped in bogs with which the ground
is covered in some parts. But we enjoyed a near
view of some grand old rocks, which form the greatest
attraction of the landscape, and which are named
" Las peñas cargadas." Dangerous though the road

was, I think we were well repaid for our perseverance. We saw the two snow-capped volcanoes shining in all their beauty. I had no idea before of the height of these two mountains, and am not a little surprised to find they both overtop Mont Blanc by nearly 2000 feet. The excessive clearness of the atmosphere renders it easy to deceive the eye. Popocatapetl and Iztaccihuatl both, but especially the former, look as if there would be no difficulty whatever in riding up to the top in a couple of hours; yet the base of the nearer of the two is forty miles off!

20*th.*—Went into one of the silver mines called the Rosario. This is cut through the side of the hill, and consequently we were able to explore it without the inconvenience of being swung down in baskets or having to climb up rope ladders. We were sent in, or rather drawn in, by a mule in a sort of truck or wheelbarrow, in which we lay down as nearly flat as we could, with candles in our hands, and were so trundled on for about a quarter of a mile. We were enveloped from head to foot in white flannel drawers and gowns, and I should think we must have looked very like a party of criminals being drawn to execution. The Rosario is now the richest of the Real del Monte mines — at least so I am told. The miners seem by no means uncomfortable, and lead a merry life, hammering away at the silvery rock, and singing all manner of songs, comic and sentimental. They gave us some of their pulque to drink, which

this time we did not think so bad.   We also obtained
leave, with the aid of a chisel and hammer, to hew
for ourselves some specimens of the ore.

21st.—Took leave of our hosts at Real del Monte
with much regret.   We have made a delightful
excursion and a most agreeable visit, to which the
only drawback has been its brief duration.   We were
obliged to leave Mr. Auld's house at half-past four
o'clock this morning, in order to be in time for a
diligence which was to pass though Pachuca at six.
The air was freezing: I don't think I ever suffered
such bitter cold before.   This time from Pachuca
we availed ourselves of the "silver escort," as some
bars were being sent on to Mexico, which we therefore
accompanied.   Our journey was accomplished without any remarkable incident, and we reached the
city in safety this evening.   The weather being fine
to-day, I was able to observe what previously had
escaped me in the hurried gallop across the plain in
the storm — namely, the numbers of large aloes or
magueys, as their Mexican name is, scattered in profusion all over the country.   Some few were in
flower, but they are rare, as immediately the owner
finds his maguey is about to blossom, he cuts its
head off for the sake of the pulque which is then in
the long stem ready to nourish the flower, but which
more generally he prefers should nourish him.

Ever your affectionate,

C.

CHAPTER XXIII.

Mexico, October 24th.—The last two mornings, my
dear Father, have been almost exclusively devoted to
visiting the public buildings, churches, &c.   On
Sunday we went to the College of the Biscayunos, a
most excellent institution, and which I should have
much regretted leaving Mexico without seeing.   The
college is a spacious, airy, and handsome edifice,
modelled, I understand, after the royal palace at
Madrid.   The founders were three rich old Biscayans
who bethought them of using their large fortune in
this charitable manner.   The college is for the benefit of girls.   They are chosen by directors or trustees
named for the purpose, and the preference is given
in election to those of Biscayan birth or descent.
When once elected the girls are taken into the
college, a magnificent and extensive building, where
they receive a good and careful education.   When
grown up they have the choice of three things,
namely, to marry, to go into a convent, or to stay
where they are as teachers.   When they choose

either of the first two vocations, they are dowried
with four thousand piastres. The internal organisation of the establishment is curious. They are divided
into little governments or republics consisting of
ten members in each. These ten possess a kitchen,
a *salon*, and a dormitory between them. They do
everything for themselves, each girl in rotation
taking her turn daily at the different employments.
One of this "council of ten" is appointed president
or governor for a month, when she goes out of office
and is succeeded by another, and so on. The system,
I understand, works admirably in every respect. On
leaving here we proceeded to the Cathedral, which,
though I had cursorily visited already, I wished to
go over again. *D'abord*, we had to take off our
bonnets and leave them in the carriage, as women
are not allowed to enter the Mexican churches in
either bonnets or hats; so we substituted scarfs en-
veloping both head and shoulders, mantilla fashion,
and so entered. The interior does not, at least now,
correspond with the grandeur of its external appearance; but, like many other things, it is sadly shorn of
its ancient glories. There is still a great deal of
silver about it, and the pillars near the high altar are
curiously enriched with many-coloured marbles; but
the aisles and body of the church are all but stripped,
and bear visible marks of popular and profane touch.
The church is of Gothic architecture, finely shaped,

G

and of immense size. Two stately towers flank the façade at either side.   Were there, however, nothing attractive either in sculpture or ornament, the Cathedral of Mexico must always possess an undying interest for the antiquary, and indeed, I should think, for all readers of history.   On the spot now hallowed by the Christian church, stood once the temple dedicated to the gods of the most revolting and cruel faith that ever stained the annals of a people since the creation of the world,—the Aztec war-deity, to whom this temple was especially devoted, and in whose honour whole hecatombs of miserable human victims were yearly sacrificed.   The present pavement of the Cathedral is entirely formed of the numerous statues and busts of their various pagan deities, notwithstanding which there are lots still to be seen at the Museum and elsewhere.   As we left the building our attention was directed to the famous Calendar stone, called in Mexican slang "el relox de Montezuma" (Montezuma's watch). In the days of the Aztec emperors it stood in the centre of the Grand Plaza, but has since been transferred to the enclosure by the Cathedral.   It is of circular form, and of great size and weight — upwards of fifty tons, I am told — and is inscribed with all manner of signs and hieroglyphics, by which means they formed a tolerably accurate computation of the lapse of time, seasons, &c.   Strange that such civi-

lisation as this should have existed at the same period with the frightful barbarities before mentioned!
Being now in proper costume for church visiting, we
took the opportunity of going to two others—namely,
San Francisco and Santa Clara. The former is one
of the most beautifully ornamented in the whole
city. Fine sculptures in variegated marble are to be
observed all around, while the altar glitters with
jewels and gold. Santa Clara is less splendid, but in
purer and better taste; white marble columns relieved with gleams of gold in the bas-reliefs. We
now drove a few miles out of Mexico to see those
curious relics of bygone days — or at least what remains of them — the *chinampas*, or floating islands.
The latter term is certainly now a misnomer. They
have all but completely attached themselves to the
continent or parent soil. In two or three instances
only a kind of rivulet or stream surrounds them, and
allows one to imagine what they might once have
been—flowery sort of rafts skimming along the quiet
surface of the lakes. I should suppose that the
interwoven aquatic plants which originally formed
the foundation of these chinampas must have thrown
out offshoots and branches which, in process of time,
encountered others from the mainland, and so knit
themselves together that in most cases the residents
on the soil even cannot tell where the mainland ends
and where the islands begin. The present appear-

ance of those we saw resembled patches of good productive kitchen garden, but lacked the wilderness of flowers. The Museum being now reopened, we went there for a couple of hours yesterday morning. There is such a strong family likeness in all museums, that it would only be tedious to enumerate any portion of the contents of this. Suffice it to say, therefore, that here are the usual statues, busts, torsos, &c., "supposed to be" of everybody; bits of gold, silver, copper, iron, lead, and all the known metals; spitted scorpions, centipedes and spiders, pickled snakes and stuffed monkeys; also a series of portraits of the Viceroys down to the days of the Republic. One natural curiosity there is worth all the other objects, in my opinion. This is "el arbol de las manitas,"— Anglicè, the tree of the little hands,— a most extraordinary plant. The flower is red, and in shape something like an anemone; but from it there protrudes a singularly correct and well-formed hand, the only difference between it and the human member being that this possesses five fingers besides a very perfect thumb. There are now, I am told, but two specimens of this plant remaining in Mexico or in the world, so that it is no matter of wonder to find it honoured by a place in the Museum. Hence we proceeded to the church attached to a charitable institution called the Hospital de Jesus. Here was the last resting-place of Cortez, if indeed the term

rest can be applied to aught which has undergone so
many changes. After being transported from Seville,
where he died, here to the land he won, his remains
were successively interred in three different places;
at Tezcuco, at the church of San Francisco in
Mexico, and lastly at this place, " Jesus of Nazareth."
To the disgrace of the Mexican mob, on the occasion
of the popular outbreak in 1823, they broke into the
church with the intention of desecrating the tomb
and destroying the remains of the hero, but for
whose life and deeds of bravery and perseverance
these wretched miscreants could not have called the
" Queen of the Valley " their own native land.   Fortunately for the Mexican reputation, timely warning
was conveyed to one of the nobles of the despicable
project of the rabble, and the ashes of Cortez were
once more disinterred and conveyed to a place of
safety.   But where that is, no one knows but the
chief actor in the scene and his family.   The secret ·
is very prudently still preserved, as the general good
order and tranquillity are by no means improving
with regard to Mexico or the Mexicans.   In the evening we attended a great ball given in the Lonja or
Exchange Room, a very brilliant affair.   Diamonds
were worn to an amount I should have thought incredible.   I was chiefly glad of this ball taking place
while we were in Mexico, by its affording me an
opportunity of seeing and having time to examine

the President Santa Anna, who, with his young wife, " assisted " at the fête. They were both seated on chairs of state raised on a velvet-covered platform, and were surrounded by the staff, ministers, corps diplomatique, officers, &c. He is a sallow-complexioned, careworn-looking man, and no wonder. I should think his life anything but an easy or an enviable one. He gives me the impression of being a man of strong determination, not easy temper, and whose will it might be dangerous to thwart. Madame Santa Anna is young and pretty — reported beautiful, but this I think an exaggeration; at least she disappointed me. Her complexion is pale, eyes and hair dark, features tolerable; but this sort of face is no uncommon one. She is of low birth, but has had the virtue to accept Santa Anna's addresses only on the condition of becoming his wife. She pays the usual penalty, however, for marrying a man more than double her age, in becoming the object of his ever watchful jealousy and suspicion. The dancing continued till nearly five o'clock in the morning, principally the " Spanish dances " so called, a kind of slow floating movement to a sort of Sir Roger de Coverley figure. Waltzes and polkas were occasionally interspersed; but the truth is, no lungs can stand quick motion through the air here, whether in running or dancing or any positive *self-*

exertion of body : the atmosphere being so rarefied, one turn of a waltz sets every one panting as if they had got the asthma.   So the Spanish dances are likely to maintain their supremacy on a stronger ground than the caprice of changeable fashion.

CHAPTER XXIV.

BEING very tired after last night's dissipation, we contented ourselves, this afternoon, with a ride on horseback a few miles out of town, where we were quiet
spectators of a very curious scene, viz. a sale of
horses, which had to be *caught* for inspection when
chosen.   I was much amused and interested with the
whole ceremony, some of the incidents of which were
most laughable. · It would be scarcely possible for
an uninitiated person, or one who had not been an
eye-witness of the performance, to understand from
a description, however minute, the extraordinary
skill of the Mexicans in throwing the lasso.   I think,
perhaps the most incomprehensible part is the apparent slowness and composure with which it gradually uncoils on its route.   A good aim, quickly and
suddenly taken, whether with a stone, a ball, or anything else, is simple enough; but the lasso, to all appearance, aims at nothing.   I repeatedly saw—that
is, I fancied I saw—the treacherous cord unrolling
itself at about the same pace as the horse was going,

keeping, as it were, alongside of him until the moment decreed by fate had arrived. Then it depended much on the character of the horse what happened afterwards. If he was of a philosophical, easy-going turn, his pace gradually slackened, and, without any violence, he was brought up for examination. If, on the other hand, and as most frequently happened, he resisted the indignity of being in any way shackled, he speedily measured his length on the ground; yet so quietly and gently withal, that his uppermost feeling, I imagine, must be astonishment even more than rage. It is certainly an exemplification of the old saw that "practice makes perfect." The men here practise it perpetually. The lasso is an indispensable accessory to every saddle, and they experimentalise on everything. Nothing comes amiss. Children, too, from their infancy, will make a slip-knot with any bit of string they can get hold of, and set to lassoing their chickens, ducks, kittens, puppies, toys, or whatever may come in their way. From this peculiarity, as may be supposed, the existence of domestic animals does not flow on so easily as it might do. I have often, from my balcony here, watched and laughed at the distress of some maternal hen, and the clucking indignation of paterfamilias at the sudden bereavement of one of their progeny by the whipcord of some mischievous urchin. The trial, to be sure, is of short duration but must

be very unpleasant to the parties concerned for the
time being.   I have also profited by this comparatively idle day, by doing a little Mexican shopping;
that is to say, I intended to do so, but unfortunately
I find, on examination, that the prices of the articles
I particularly desired were quite beyond my *portée.*
The principal object of my ambition, in the way of
personal decoration, was a genuine Spanish mantilla
made of blonde, either black or white, such as I see
les grandes dames of Mexico are in the habit of
wearing; but on selecting one which pleased me, and
inquiring its price, I heard, to my consternation, that
it amounted to 200 dollars, *i. e.* upwards of 40*l.*   So,
as anything like that sum was out of the question,
I ceased to think any more about it.   I have, however, succeeded in obtaining two very handsome
specimens of the Mexican "serape," which I shall
send to you the first opportunity, or, if none presents
itself, I shall keep and bring home with me.   They
are, at all events, uncommon, and not to be seen
every day.   The only thing against them is, that
though they will make capital railway wraps, and
effectually preserve you from both dust and cold,
they are so singular in form, and the colours so many
and so brilliant, that I almost fear you might render
yourself liable to be taken up, or mistaken for the
Pope or the Sultan, or some equally mischievous
person.   I have also bought two or three silver

brooches, principally used by the Mexicans to fasten their sombreros, or rather the feathers or ribands they may wear in them. These brooches are specially interesting as bearing for their design the national emblem, namely, an eagle flying, wings extended, and carrying in his claws a large branch of the nopal or prickly pear. These, together with a Mexican riding whip and some *valentines* (oddly enough, they have the custom, though not the day, here; and whereas we make ours the 14th of February, they make theirs on the day we devote to geese, the 29th of September), are, I think, all the extravagances of which I have been guilty. This letter, I see, has extended itself to a most unconscionable length; therefore, as I do not wish to ruin you in postage, I shall now conclude, and remain

Your ever affectionate

C.

CHAPTER XXV.

Mexico, Oct. 26th.—My dear Father,—This will, I fear
be the last or nearly the last letter you will receive
from me dated Mexico, for the time of our departure
is now drawing very near.   The actual day is not yet
fixed, as it will greatly depend upon circumstances,
about which I will tell you when all is finally ar-
ranged and I know myself what our movements will
be.   Yesterday we went to Tacuba, the ancient
Tlacopan, and the spot to which Cortez retreated
after the first great reverse that befel the Spanish
arms after the conquest.   We followed step by step
the same path taken by the routed troops on that
"noche triste," or sad night, and lingered for a few
minutes at the scene of the famous leap of Alvarado,
who, finding himself cut off from all hope of retreat,
alone against countless enemies, took the desperate
measure of planting his lance firmly in the bottom
of the stream, and by its aid swung himself across a
prodigious distance out of reach of his assailants.
There is at Tacuba now a small field with some old

trees and flowering rose-bushes. Under one of the
former, called by his name, Cortez is said to have
passed the dark hours of that dreary night. I
gathered a bunch of the roses to keep as a souvenir
of the spot for my own satisfaction; but for a narration of this most extraordinary and romantic·episode
in the history of those days, it would be the height
of presumption in any one to attempt it after the
account given in the incomparably eloquent pages of
Prescott. Spent the evening with the same friends
whom we visited at Tacuba some weeks ago, and
who have now come into Mexico for the winter.
Had tea *à l'Anglaise*, and what was far better, at
least for a change, chocolate *à la Mexicaine*. It
would be impossible to imagine anything more
delicious in its way than chocolate as they prepare
it in this country. Without of course instancing
England, where by asking you get a cup of what
is libellously called chocolate and in taste approxi-
mates to toast and water mixed with sky-blue milk
and sweetened with syrup, I will compare the chocolate
here with what is given you in France, where they
flatter themselves they understand the beverage; yet
I have no hesitation in saying that even the French
know nothing about the matter. In the more
absorbing attraction of other incidents of our journey
between Vera Cruz and this city, I find I have
been ungrateful enough to omit any mention of the

sustenance afforded us by the chocolate, always found in perfection and in plenty at the poorest and humblest huts on the road. I remember particularly, on the occasion I have already mentioned, when, in the middle of a cold, rainy, stormy night, our diligence stuck fast in some of the deep ruts abounding in the way, we entered what appeared to be nothing better than a hovel of the most miserable description. The inside did not either at all belie the promise of the out. In one room, or rather portion of space, unpartitioned, were sleeping a man and woman, two children, two goats, a pig, a parrot, a cat, a lot of poultry roosting in the oddest places, and dogs *ad libitum;* besides dried fruit, vegetables, meat, &c., hanging from the rafters on the roof. It might be naturally supposed that in a place of this description one would find nothing superexcellent in the way of *cuisine;* and yet, within ten minutes of our unlooked-for *entrée* in their cabin, these hospitable Indians produced a potful of hot chocolate, the like of which I would challenge all Paris to equal. To return to our friend's *soirée* after this digression: we occupied our evening in playing *vingt-et-un,* which, by the way, is the general nightly amusement here, and much more resorted to than dancing — I suppose for the reasons I mentioned in describing the Lonja ball. This morning, Eleanor not being actively inclined, I rode with Mr. Berkeley to San Augustin, a village

some eight miles from here, which is actually devoted
to no other purpose than that of gambling.   Curious
country and still more curious government, where
the existence of such a state of things as an institution is permitted!   The gambling fêtes for this year
are over now (they take place in June); but though
for the present deserted, my cicerone pointed out to
me the various houses where so many fortunes change
hands, besides describing to me the details of what
takes place, he having been a visitor annually for
some time past.   The principal and favourite game
is "Monte," which, as far as I can make out, differs
very little if at all from Lansquenet; but the merry-
making once begun, both sexes, all ranks, the young
and the old, the rich and the poor, crowd to San
Augustin, and play with, against, and beside each
other.   I am sorry to add that the affections of this
heterogeneous multitude are equally divided, or
nearly so, between Monte and a far more inhuman
amusement, namely, cock-fighting; the slaughter of
these poor innocents at the annual fêtes amounts to
something enormous, the fashion of fastening sharp
knives to their spurs preventing any chance of preserving their lives, with very few exceptions.   An
absurd story is told, and I believe well authenticated,
of the President Santa Anna, whose excessive love for
cock-fighting once led him into most irreverent and
uncourteous behaviour to a Mexican bishop.   The

latter had gone to call on Santa Anna by appoint-
ment, but the conversation had scarcely begun when
the President started up and left the room. The
reverend padre waited for some time patiently, then
wonderingly. At length he rang the bell, and, in
answer to his inquiries, was told that Santa Anna
" had gone to visit a sick friend." " Who ? " "Silvertail." " Who is Silvertail ? " " His excellency's
favourite gamecock, who was wounded in a fight this
morning ! "

CHAPTER XXVI.

October 28*th.* — This is our very last day in Mexico, my dear Father. I therefore yield to the temptation of dating yet one more letter from it, though probably my despatch will not be closed till we are some way on the return route. We shall reach Vera Cruz some days before the steamer, but by taking our departure now, although it is a little premature, we shall have the double advantage of an escort the whole way, and also we shall enjoy the company of our friends the Riberas. Madame de Ribera is going to Europe with her child, and Monsieur accompanies her as far as Vera Cruz, where a Spanish man-of-war awaits her embarkation. The whole of this afternoon has been occupied in preparations for our journey and in receiving numerous farewell visits. We have found many good friends here from whom we shall separate with great regret. . . . . . Yesterday morning at a very early hour we left Mexico on an expedition to a place called " El Desierto," *anglicè*, the desert. Why so called it would be difficult to determine, for

nothing could very well be more unlike our general
notions of a desert.   It is about fourteen miles from
Mexico.   For the first time I thought the view
to-day, as we gradually approached our destination,
fully equalled the description of the valley given by
so many chroniclers, from Cortez to Humboldt.
Hills, valleys, lakes, and mountains outvied each
other, shining under a purple sky, and almost realised the dreams of the olden time.   We left our
carriage at the village of Toluca, and shortly after
commenced the ascent of a steep hill leading to the
" desierto."   It was formerly a monastery, but is
now used as a glass manufactory.   Every step we
took disclosed views, the one only more exquisitely
beautiful than the other.   Much as I have seen to
admire and to enchant in this wonderful country, this
day's excursion has surpassed all.   It was decreed by
the fates that we should not return without an adventure ; for we had no sooner begun to wend our
way down the little path leading back to Toluca, than
the most violent storm of tropical rain that can be
imagined burst over our heads.   It really, as they say
in Yorkshire, " came heaven down."   We were wet
through in two minutes ; but this was not the worst
part of the business.   The ground, which had previously been parched and burnt from a long con-
tinuance of dry weather now became so slippery with
the rain, which had glazed more than soaked the

soil, that it was quite impossible to keep one's footing at all; and so slipping, sliding, stumbling and
falling, we pursued our downward course.   However,
" all's well that ends well;" we *did* arrive at last, drove
home, and happily accomplished our expedition
without even catching cold.   This morning we took
our last ride on horseback; went to see the tree
hallowed by the " noche triste."   .   .   .   .

.   .   .   .

Puebla, Oct. 29th.—I resume my letter. We reached
here about an hour ago. We had to get up at a
dreadful hour this morning, starting at four o'clock ;
cold and miserable, and so we bid a sad farewell to
Mexico.   Our companions are Monsieur and Madame de Ribera, their little boy, and a wonderful
old woman, upwards of seventy, who is returning to
Spain after having passed her whole life from the
age of sixteen in Mexico. Some one of her relations
has died and left her a fortune in her old age. So
she is now about to go and end her days in her
own country. Not a wise plan, I think, as she is far
too aged to find old or make new friends now in old
Spain, whereas she leaves the ties and associations of
half a century behind her.   Madame de Ribera was
nursing with tender care two extraordinary little dogs
of the Chihuahua* breed.   They are at present only

* Pronounced Chi-wa-wa.

in their early puppy-hood, and are of the size of very small kittens; but their full growth scarcely attains that of a common domestic cat. Most marvellous tales are told concerning the manners and customs of this race of canines, for the truth of which of course I cannot vouch, knowing nothing of the matter. They say these dogs are met with in and surrounding the Chihuahua part of Mexico; that their organisation is a sort of " United States " in miniature, only that, with the quadrupedal republic, they have the advantage of a " president " to each state, and that president is — a rattle snake! They are said, nevertheless, to live in a state of exemplary order and felicity, a kind of Utopian mixture of free trade and protection, the former consisting of a course of " trading " carried on by the dogs in a manner more free than welcome, and the latter, as may be guessed, afforded by the snakes on principles which Mr. Cobden himself I imagine would accede to. Unlike political parties, however, there exists honour among thieves here. The dogs forage for the snakes, as well as themselves, and the snakes in their turn defend the dogs from all adversaries, and do not, according to the manner of " liberals " and " conservatives," desert their friends. Madame de Ribera's little charges are amusing and affectionate little things, not old enough yet to have felt any filial affection for their formidable parent. I nursed one all the way, it having ensconced itself

very comfortably in my neck, between my bonnet and
cloak.   Among other methods of whiling away the
long hours of our journey, I derive great amusement,
besides instruction, in the Spanish language by listening to the prattle of the young Ribera, a fine merry
child of about seven years old.   True Castilian is undeniably the queen or empress of languages, and from
the lips of a child sounds peculiarly beautiful.   Soft,
without the namby pamby drawl of Italian, grand,
without the harshness of German, and brilliant, without the sharpness of French.   One expression particularly amuses me in this little fellow: when he
differs in opinion with his father, or means to remon-
strate with him, he exclaims, in such a dignified
manner, " Hombre !"   It is a very common Spanish
expression, and means a great deal, though its
literal translation is merely "man!" which sounds
odd enough from a child to his father; but it is equivalent to a long English sentence: for instance, " But,
my dear Sir, I assure you, you're quite wrong; only
reflect for a moment," &c., would all be expressed by
the Spanish "Hombre!"

CHAPTER XXVII.

PUEBLA.

WE have passed over the same ground as in coming, only that we reached here earlier in the day, and consequently have had an opportunity of judging a little more of the town, which is remarkably handsome, and of visiting the cathedral. This is a most beautiful edifice, far superior in all respects, I think (size excepted), to that of Mexico. The church was so quickly built that tradition says the workmen were helped by angels, who came by night and advanced their work. Hence the name by which Puebla is distinguished, namely, " Puebla de los Angeles." . . . A few hours after penning the above lines, we again set out on our journey, another night and part of a day bringing us to Perote, which looked much less dismal than on our first visit. We had the loveliest view ever since daybreak of the two Mexican volcanoes, and towards the close, in the glorious light of the setting sun, Orizava burst upon our sight. Next morning, in due course of time, we reached beautiful Jalapa again. The scenery, trees, and flowers seem to me even more wonderful, if possible, than on my first visit. Nothing I have ever seen, heard, or read of has equalled this in colouring. It is quite indescribable, and would only seem to be exaggeration were I to attempt to render the impression the whole scene leaves on the mind and memory.

We remained the whole day at Jalapa, reserving the uninteresting Tierra Caliente between it and Vera Cruz for traversing at night. Having refreshed ourselves with an excellent *déjeûner à la fourchette*, we took a long walk with our friends into the country, and returned laden with floripundias and roses. On our way back we entered some of the cottages scattered around. In one of these we unexpectedly came upon a most interesting group. A picturesque-looking young Mexican playing the guitar and singing to his lady-love; she, the while occupied in twining bright flowers in her hair! I thought those days of romance had gone by; and so they have in the mother country, since "Cervantes laughed Spain's chivalry away;" but here they are less civilised! Another night ended our land journey without any accident, and brought us to Vera Cruz, whence I am at this moment writing (Nov. 6th), having arrived here three days ago. We have had a most unexpectedly pleasant sojourn at Vera Cruz. It certainly exemplifies the truth of the proverb about giving a dog a bad name. This much maligned town has the reputation of being dull, dismal, and disagreeable in every respect, and we anticipated spending our three or four days of detention about as profitably as if we had been in quarantine; whereas, thanks partly to Mr. Giffard (the consul), who has introduced us to some friends of his residing here, we have had riding horses placed at our disposition by different people each day, and have enjoyed ourselves exceedingly. As soon as the town and the immediately surrounding sands of Vera Cruz are passed, you enter into the most charming country scenery in the world. We cantered about for miles over green turf, and through green lanes and leafy glades worthy of England itself. Indeed I was quite forcibly reminded of Wonersh, only that, besides all the beautiful green verdure to be seen there, flowers grow here such as England dreams not of. An odd adventure, which might have proved a catastrophe, occurred to us yesterday. An old Mexican gentleman, Señor G——, had begged to be chosen purveyor of our steeds for the day, and accordingly at 3 o'clock two magnificent looking horses were at our door. They did not seem pleased at our mounting, but that we thought nothing of, and all went well till we were outside the town gates, on the sand-hills immediately surrounding them. Here our horses began to *perform*. Eleanor's *bolted* at once, and she threw herself off, very fortunately clearing the saddle, and as she fell on soft sand was not hurt. My steed meanwhile began to plunge in the most frightful manner I ever saw; but I was afraid to throw myself off, so on him I sat, till, suddenly, the saddle turned round and I fell. By great good luck the horse made a great bound off without touching me, so I was *quitte pour la peur;* and after all we managed to get our ride not on these bucephali, but on a couple of steady "sage" ponies lent us by some one else. But the cream of the incident was this. The old gentleman on being questioned on the subject, very coolly said, "No one had ever *mounted* these horses before, but that he had always understood it to be a matter of indifference to English women what 'wild beasts' they rode!" I must now bring my last Mexican letter to a close, though we shall travel to Havana together; but as the vessel will only remain there a few hours, I probably should not have time to write on arriving there. So adieu,

Your ever affectionate

C.

CHAPTER XXVIII.

Havana, November 11*th.*—My dear Father, — We
embarked on the same evening on which I closed my
letter at Vera Cruz. A furious "norte" blowing, I
thought we should have been swamped several times
before reaching the steamer. The waves dashed all
over us, and we were completely drenched when we
at length arrived. The gale became worse as the
day wore on, and at last the shore boats asked a
hundred dollars for bringing or taking any one from
the land to the vessel or *vice versâ*. These "nortes"
or northerly gales are the terrors of the Mexican ·
Gulf. They come on generally without any warning,
and like the Provençal mistral, they last either three
or nine days, and cause for the most part great
damage, besides doubly adding to the dangers of the
Alacranes. Unfortunately our gale was one of the
nine days' duration, consequently we have had a long
and most disagreeable passage — rough sea, bad ship,
and worse accommodation. The Avon is the name
of the packet and as far as I have yet seen it is

the only really bad and uncomfortable one in the
West India service. You may imagine under these
circumstances what a relief it was, to make Havana at
last, to see the dear old "ace of clubs" again (i. e. the
harbour of Havana which is shaped exactly like one),
and to meet our good Spanish friends once more.

15th. — Yesterday evening we dined at the Quin-
ton with the captain-general, and met a large
party of hidalgos and official grandees, with their
señoras and señoritas; that is, in more humble words
than the grandiloquent Spanish, their wives and
daughters. I suppose it is in consequence of so little
being heard or known in general society, now-a-days,
of Spain or the Spaniards, so few names now rise
to the surface so as to be saved from the waters of
oblivion; and even these few are rarely known to any
but the small party constituting the *crême de la
crême* of different nations; that on hearing mentioned in presentation to me, those of Villa Hermosa,
Pinalves, Fernandina, Velasquez, Alva, Alvarez, Xime-
nes, &c., I was for a short time almost bewildered,
wondering whether I had gone back to school days
and was brushing up my history, or whether I had
fallen into a reverie over the chronicles of the Cid or
Don Quixote. It was all real, however, and a most
agreeable and sociable party; but so I find all
General Cañedo's are. His *receptions* are on the plan
of most royal levées and similar ceremonies; yet,

strange to say, here in Cuba the regal or vice-regal
audiences are far less serious affairs than a private
"morning call."   With the captain-general, when you
have properly gone through the ceremony of making
your reverence to the representative of Queen Isabel,
you may do whatever you please, walk about, change
your place, in short, amuse yourself as fancy leads you.
But with the Cuban nobility and gentlefolks it is
quite another affair.   I remember receiving a very
strong impression on this subject from one of the
first visits I paid in Havana, namely, to the Count and
Countess O'Reilly, to whom Isturiz had "addressed
me."   I was shown into a large barren-looking room
(but from the windows of which there was a most
heavenly view), the only furniture which was visible
— and that most alarmingly so — being a dozen
rocking chairs ranged in two rows opposite each
other.   La Senora Condesa received me, seated in
one of these machines, and placed me next her.   By
and by, in walked some junior members (*males*) of
the family; they planted themselves just opposite, and
we all began to talk; but it was in vain to try
and turn the conversation to some less engrossing
subject than how or where we had all spent our
morning.   I think I must have got what the French
call an *attaque de nerfs*.   At last I remarked on the
beauty of the view, the flowers, everything I could
see; and of course hoped a walk on the terrace would

be proposed.   But nothing of the sort; each male
who came in seating himself on one side and each
female on the other, till we must all have looked
like a pack of ghosts, bowing to each other.
To be sure, it was consolatory to be told everything
they possessed was mine, and entirely at my disposition; yet I would willingly have sacrificed all these
possessions " *en Espagne* " for the present power of
pushing away my rocking chair and going wherever
the spirit impelled me.   Having now been here some
time, and having had opportunities afforded me of
gaining a thorough insight into the way things are
socially conducted, I understand tolerably well the
principles on which visiting is carried on.   A call is
a state ceremony, and if you are the bearer of a letter
of introduction, the greater form and etiquette with
which you are received, the greater is the honour they
intend thereby to show you, and greater the compliment to the friend who introduces you.   Of course this
applies to the Havanese or Spanish only; other people
act according to the custom of their own country,
whatever that may be.   The excessive formality,
however, of which I have been telling is only applicable
to the first visit or morning call, as after that you are
generally invited to the evening receptions or *tertul-*
lias given by most of the Havanese families on stated
evenings.   Here you amuse yourself well enough, and
above all, as you please.   You may dance, or play

on the piano, or play at cards, or at petits-jeux.   At
each or all of these you will find companions; or, if
you are in a savage mood, you may swing in a rocking
chair, no very uncommon occupation either, and a very
decided improvement on trying to keep oneself still
on the edge of one, as befell me, as I have narrated,
on my first state visit to Countess O'Reilly. To-night
I was presented to one of the great dignitaries of the
church, namely, the Archbishop of Santiago de Cuba,
who bears the rather singular name (at least to my
ears), "Claret y Clara."   When I was a child I used
to be called, by way of a diminutive or pet name,
"Clara Claretti," so I was not a little amused at
finding the Reverendissimo Padre "answer to" my
name reversed, that is, "Claret y Clara!" The
minister of police was another of the guests who attracted my attention and wonder, the latter from his
being one of the most innocent and simple-looking
individuals I ever remember seeing.   Nor did his
manners or conversation belie the expression of his
face.   He seemed good nature and benevolence per-
sonified.   Of course, all this may be assumed; if so, he
is a consummate actor.   But I can scarcely think it;
and if he really is as kind-hearted as he looks, I should
not exactly think him qualified for the trying post
of Minister of Police in a place where, owing to the
secret machinations and insidious agents of the United
States, always at work to sow the seeds of revolt, or

blow the faintest spark of discontent into a blaze, it would seem imperatively necessary that one on whom so much *may* depend vitally affecting the island and the honour of the Spanish crown, should be no mere carpet knight, but one possessed of "the mind to will, the hand to execute." While on this subject, i.e. the constant plots and attempts at annexation carried on so unblushingly, though happily, hitherto ineffectually, by the American filibusters, I will endeavour to give you a slight sketch of the principal incidents connected with the memorable Lopez expedition.

CHAPTER XXIX.

WHATEVER difference of opinion may exist regarding the political expediency of annexation, or whatever may be argued on the one side or the other of the advantages to be gained by America, or even, as advanced by some casuists, *ultimately* to Spain, there can be but one view entertained by any right thinking or even commonly honest persons with respect to the course adopted by the States in this unhappy affair. It must redound to the eternal disgrace of the Americans, of those at least who were the movers or promoters of the scheme, that they inveigled into their toils, and chose for their tools—in this atrocious outrage on a friendly nation—not grown men who knew what they risked, knew what they did, and, whether for good or for ill, were prepared to abide the issue; not these, but young, ardent, enthusiastic boys. In some instances, mere lads of fifteen and sixteen were enticed and snared away from their homes to join in this nefarious enterprise. And under whose command were these misguided victims placed?

Under a hero, a man of honour, a man of even ordinary good faith or honesty of purpose? No: but under the orders of a traitor, a renegade soldier, false to his colours and his country, a broken and disgraced castaway from the Spanish army—General Narciso Lopez! To trace the causes which influenced, and which afterwards perhaps mainly contributed to the maturing these schemes, and their disastrous results, it will be necessary to go back to the commencement of the year 1848. The French Revolution, which had hurled Louis Philippe from his throne, had not only convulsed the whole of Europe, but had greatly added to and lent impetus to revolutionary and democratic principles in both the Old world and the New. To the demagogues of the United States, especially, no period could have been more propitious: their recent annexation of Texas had disclosed to them the sweets of stolen goods—a species of pleasure peculiarly grateful to the American sense. Added to this, some cheap and easy victories which had crowned their arms in the Mexican Republic rendered their acquisition of Cuba an "*eternal necessity*" (as a Yankee once told me in talking over the subject). They took their measures accordingly. To set the press to work to write inflammatory articles in all directions, was of course easy enough; but besides this, they hired a number of other agents, for the most part men of the worst

character, to visit the island in the guise of inoffen-
sive strangers, but who were to take every opportunity of fomenting any discontent which might
arise from natural causes; to sound the opinions, and
discover the weak points of all on whom they might
find the arts of seduction would tell: in short, to
arouse the passion of resentment and kindle rebellion
against their masters in all who were misguided
enough to listen to them.   One of the first, and
certainly the most important of the proselytes they
gained, was the famous Lopez.   This man was a
native of Venezuela, but had served from his youth
in the Spanish army.   Even after the declaration of
independence by that state, he adhered to his former
allegiance, and by his own request became a natural-
ised subject of the Spanish government, and maintained his rank as an officer in the army.   He
was, however, a few years previously (in 1841)
General Commandant of the Centre of the Island
and Governor of Trinidad.   In course of time this
was relinquished, on his being appointed President
"*de la comision militar*" of the whole island,
and this post he actually held in 1848, being
quartered in Cienfuegos at the southern part of the
country. Here took place the beginning of the end
a few years later.   Profiting by his high position,
and the consequent knowledge he possessed of the
strength as of the weakness of the government, as

well as the prestige of his own popularity, which
was considerable, he commenced the formation of
a plan, which, by the gradual and insidious corruption
of the soldiery under him, and the judicious expenditure of American dollars in bribes and other modes,
was ultimately to lead to the betrayal of his trust
and the delivery of the island to the United States.
But the old saying, "Treason never prospers," proved
itself true in this instance, as in many others.   Information was conveyed by some unknown hand to
the then Governor of Trinidad of the conspiracy and
its chief promoter, and measures were promptly
taken for the arrest of Lopez in the first instance.
He too, however, received timely warning and succeeded in escaping to the States.   A military com-
mission was held immediately, at which all circumstances connected with the plot were discovered.
It had not then spread very far, nor were the arrange-
ments sufficiently matured to cause for the time
being many fears for the future.   Lopez was tried
by court martial, broken and disgraced from the
army, and condemned to death as guilty of high
treason and rebellion.   Thus matters stood (with
the further discovery and discomfiture of another
though less important combination in the following
November) at the close of 1848.   The ensuing year,
1849, passed in comparative tranquillity, disturbed
only at one period by the news of a society being

organised in Rhode Island for the old story. This, however, was publicly discouraged by the President of the United States (General Taylor), its dispersion ordered — a further enactment that it should be declared "piracy," with all the attendant pains and penalties, in whomsoever should make any fresh attempts on Cuba. This slight interlude of peace was soon to be troubled: 1850, which had dawned auspiciously, was speedily to be shadowed by the dark cloud of war and tumult, and, worse still, of pestilence; and even this last scourge the unfortunate Cubans owed, under Heaven's permission, to the Americans. During the two preceding years the southern portion of the North American continent had terribly suffered from the ravages of cholera; yet, thanks to the general precautions taken all over the island, Cuba had so far escaped contagion. Towards the close of the month of March a few isolated cases only presented themselves in the military hospital of Havana, but in the course of a few short weeks the epidemic rapidly increased, and by the middle of May the mortality had attained an average of 125 to 150 a day in Havana alone. It was in this deplorable state of affairs, and when the attention and energies of all were directed to alleviating the sufferings of the sick, and warding off as far as might be the approaches of disease from the comparatively small number of places that were as yet unscathed, that

the first serious invasion, under the auspices of
Lopez, was accomplished. On the 19th of May
he surprised the town of Cardénas just before daybreak, and effected a landing, together with five hundred companions. It seems very extraordinary
that Cardénas, though a seaport, and possessing a
population of 3500 souls, should have been indebted to a guard of seventeen men only for
the first desperate resistance the invaders encountered. They fought gallantly, however, though
against impossible odds ; they intrenched themselves
in four houses, and only after eleven of their little
band being killed or wounded, and the houses they
had barricaded set fire to, they succumbed. But
they had already succeeded in gaining the ines-
timable benefit of time. The obstinate defence
they had made had lasted several hours, and had
enabled a few sturdy townspeople, who had not lost
their wits with alarm, to summon assistance from the
neighbourhood. The great majority of the inhabitants, I am told, however, were so horror-struck,
partly with fear, and partly with surprise, at their
morning slumbers being thus so rudely broken, that
they became as if paralysed, and either barred themselves up in their own houses, leaving the public
buildings to the mercy of the depredators, or else, as
occurred in many instances, fled precipitately into
the country, leaving all their property to its fate.

Succour was now at hand : towards the close of the
day some strong reinforcements of regular troops
from Matanzas and elsewhere poured into the
beleaguered town. These were also aided further by a
small band of the neighbouring peasantry, who
armed and placed themselves under the command of
the regular officers. A hand to hand fight now took
place, which resulted in the total rout of the enemy,
who were driven back in confusion to their boats,
and under cover of the night made good their escape,
together, unfortunately, with the traitor Lopez. The
next morning the extent of injury incurred by the
town was verified, of which it may truly be said, it is
well it was no worse. The churches, rich houses
and public buildings, generally, were despoiled of
whatever ornaments, or objects of value they contained. Moreover Lopez, " qui s'y connaissait,"
contrived to " abstract " a considerable quantity of
money from the custom house and the Fondo de las
obras Publicas (an establishment answering to the
French Hôtels de Villes), both of which edifices he
completely ransacked. The news of the attack, and
its signal defeat, was now quickly conveyed to
Havana. The people concerned seemed to have been
too busy to think of taking or sending any information at the time; at least, it was certainly not known
in Havana till the next day, and then singularly
enough, almost simultaneously with the Cardénas

history, there entered the harbour a Spanish war-
steamer, called the Pizarro, commanded by a
Captain Armero, bringing with him between fifty
and sixty prisoners he had fished up in Yucatan.
They gave this account of themselves: that they had
started with Lopez, intending to join in the attack
on Cardénas, but had repented *en route*, and consequently had been set on shore in Yucatan and left
to their fate. Sad and melancholy, as was the
general aspect of Havana at this time of disease and
trouble, the intelligence of this double event, caused
an universal and spontaneous demonstration of
enthusiasm and goodwill to the government. The
prisoners brought in the Pizarro were mostly
liberated, with the exception of three or four, but
who afterwards received a free pardon from the
Queen.   On the old principle of shutting the stable-
door when the steed was stolen (which proverb by
the bye is of Spanish origin) measures were now
taken throughout the island for an organised system
of defence. No great difficulty certainly presented
itself. In an incredibly short time, upwards of
13,000 men enrolled themselves in the volunteer
service of the Government; 3000 muskets were
distributed by the Captain-General in Havana, and
the remaining 10,000 volunteers were formed into
four battalions which were variously distributed
about the country. The style and title of " Nobles

Vecinos" * were given them. There were hopes now entertained that, tired and discouraged by the successive failures which had been their lot, the filibusters would at last give way, and Cuba be left in peace. To a certain extent these hopes were fulfilled; a little breathing time at least was enjoyed. In the meanwhile the governor of the island † was relieved from the post he had filled during this troubled period. He was succeeded by General Concha, one of the most popular captains-general, from all accounts, that have ever wielded the vice-regal sceptre here. For his administration was reserved the honour of defeating the last and most important attack yet made by the Annexation party, of crushing for ever the career of Lopez and the few Spanish adherents he had gained, and this, notwithstanding the success which, for the first three days, attended them; and finally of reading a lesson to the Americans, which it is to be hoped will not be lost upon them, teaching them how, by their unconquerable love of wrong and robbery, they have not only delivered over to famine, disease, imprisonment, and death, — inglorious and shameful death, — the numbers of brave and thoughtless boys, the account of whose sufferings forms one of the most painful episodes in this sad history; but they have lowered themselves

---

* Literally, "noble neighbours."
† General Roncali, Comte de Alcoy.

in the estimation of mankind, disgraced the stars and stripes in the eyes of surrounding nations. Yes, "repudiate" as they may, they have connived at and allowed that flag to afford protection to as desperate a gang of pirates and banditti as ever crossed a sea or devastated a land. I am, however, rather forestalling events, and must now endeavour to relate, in their proper order, the various incidents as they occurred, from the first alarm being sounded in the summer of the year 1851.

CHAPTER XXX.

On the 11th of August of that year, Lopez disembarked at a place called El Morrillo near Bahia Honda, a short distance to the west of Havana. His force amounted on this occasion to about 450, but nearly half of these consisted of the youthful victims I have before alluded to. He directed his steps in the first instance, with about 300 of his followers, to the little village of Las Pozas; the remaining portion of them being left in charge of the baggage and provisions, with orders to join themselves to the main body at the earliest opportunity consistent with safety. Meanwhile, unlike the former occasion, the news had spread like wildfire, and in as short a space of time as circumstances would allow, seven companies of infantry under the command of General Ena embarked from Havana and reached the scene of action, or I should rather say approached it, as for a short period they halted at Morrillo to reconnoitre the state of affairs. In talking over these things now, quietly

and at a distance, I am told, by those who are considered competent to pronounce a judgment, that
General Ena made a great mistake in not taking
more time; that, seeing how things were, and that
Lopez had been enabled during the long day of the
12th of August to most importantly improve and
strengthen his position, having managed by means of
trenches, mounds, parapets, &c. to establish a sort of
fortification; Ena should have sent for more help,
and also some guns from Havana, instead of risking
an attack under these disadvantageous circumstances.
Unfortunately, he seems, however, to have been a man
of more daring and courage than reflection; and accordingly, without waiting for what prudence might
have counselled, he ordered an impetuous assault in
the evening.   To add to the unfavourable chances, his
men were already tired, hungry, exhausted; they had
had neither rest, food, nor drink since their disem-
barkation and had waited under arms during the
whole night of the 12th.   Early on the morning then
of the 13th (having marched from Morrillo) was the
word of command given, and without one single
piece of artillery with which to return the enemy's
fire (who had well provided themselves with field
pieces), and faint in body though not in spirit, they
made a .gallant, but, as may. be supposed, fruitless
effort.   The village of Las Pozas being built something in the form of a two-pronged fork, the be-

siegers had to divide themselves into two separate
parties, and as these were composed of only two
companies each (the remaining three being left as a
corps de reserve at Morrillo), little damage was done
to the besieged.   After some desperate fighting, Ena
and his band were forced to retire; their retreat was
however most admirably managed, and, as it happened, was the means, thanks to the perfect disci-
pline and order maintained, of half retrieving the
fortune of the day.   Lopez trusting to the prestige
of this, his first and most unlooked-for success,
ordered a sortie, and an attack to be made in the
rear of the retreating Spaniards.   This was a bad
enough move; the Royal troops, having retreated
in unbroken order, now faced about; a furious hand-
to-hand fight ensued, which ended in upwards of a
hundred of the enemy being left dead or wounded on
the field.   While these events were taking place at
Las Pozas, the remaining three companies of the
Spanish soldiery, under the command of Colonel
Villaoz, who had remained in reserve at Morrillo, had
fallen upon the commissariat and baggage parties of
the filibusters, and obtained a signal success.   These
last consisted of nearly 180 men and boys.   They
were totally defeated and put to the rout: more than
half were killed and wounded on the spot; about
forty succeeded in reaching the sea and embarking
in boats, by which means ten or twelve perhaps ac-

complished a safe passage to the United States; the remainder were caught, made prisoners, tried by court martial and shot, poor wretches, with very little ceremony at Havana within a few days of their flight. Their fate, miserable as it was, however, must be considered more fortunate than much that was in store for some other of their fellow-conspirators in this eventful and ill-starred expedition. By his imprudent sortie from Las Pozas, and the severe check he there encountered, Lopez had, though late, taken warning; and, profiting by his past experience, he now decided on a sort of guerilla mode of warfare, by which he hoped to hold on until he had regathered and to some extent reorganised his scattered force. With this intention he evacuated Pozas the same day, and its terrified inhabitants might have returned to their homes; but they had already wandered away far and wide, thinking, very reasonably, that the marauders were unlikely to have left anything but desolation behind them Lopez now retired to the hills and fastnesses abounding in the Cordillera or mountain chain of the Vuelta Abajo. Here the natural difficulties in the way of attack, facilities for defence,—the character of the country rendering it inaccessible to cavalry, while immense rocks seeming as if they had suddenly sprung from the ground on purpose to afford safe ambuscade to brigands of every description,—might have well enabled a guerilla leader, who possessed the sympathies and goodwill, or even who had not incurred the opposition, of the dwellers on the soil, to maintain himself against all aggression for months or even years. But this was not the good fortune of Lopez. He had, on the contrary, provoked the hostility and let loose the indignation of all classes against him. The homes he had burnt and destroyed, the lands he had ravaged and laid waste, the blood he had shed or caused to be shed of the unoffending and helpless peasantry on whom he had descended like a thunder-bolt, the havock and ruin which everywhere marked the traces of his path, had armed every man's hand against him : there were none to help, there were all to oppose. Whatever he succeeded in obtaining, whether food or aught else, was by violence or theft. Nothing was given, nothing sold to him. War to the knife was the general and universal sentiment aroused in the hearts of all, and so the catastrophe was gradually approaching. Long, long after these events had passed and gone, things began to ooze out little by little, which showed how miserably the majority of these unlucky Americans must have been deceived, deliberately and systematically misled from the very beginning of the enterprise. They were positively assured, and *were shown letters* purporting to come from the heads of the principal families in Cuba, as well as from officers high in the army, that the whole island was prepared to rise to a man to shake off the Spanish dominion; that parties were organised, plans of action laid, a period of simultaneous action prepared and made ready, for which the signal was to be the landing of Lopez and his band: in short, that from every fort and tower the flag of Castile and Leon was to be struck, and the triumphant "Stripes and Stars" unfurled in its place! How such absurd trash should have been believed for one moment, and much more acted upon, by even the youngest and most credulous of their number, has never been made very clear; but of the misrepresentation by which they were deluded, there is no doubt. To return to my narrative : the position of the enemy being known, and, thanks to the unwavering fidelity and loyalty of the country people, General Ena and his officers being made acquainted with every movement attempted or carried into effect by the invaders, some fresh detachments of troops having been now supplied, the General proceeded to form a cordon round that part of the cordillera which sheltered the insurgents, so as to effectually close up all avenues of retreat, and, to a great degree, any possibility of changing their quarters. The consequence of this line of action became soon apparent. Want of provisions soon forced Lopez to send a foraging party from their lurking-place to seek food, or, indeed I should more correctly say, his whole body sallied forth for

this object. They had advanced as far as a Cafetal
or Coffee Plantation, called "El Cafetal de Frias,"
where they were attacked by the Royalist regiments,
commanded by General Ena in person. What the
ultimate result of this engagement might have been
under other circumstances it is impossible to say, but
the conflict had scarcely begun, indeed, the general
firing had not commenced, when the ill-fated Ena,
who had ridden to the front in order to give some
directions about the manœuvering of his men, received
a ball in his chest, and immediately dropped from his
horse. He was instantaneously carried to the rear, and
some faint hopes were entertained that the wound might
not prove mortal; but all in vain, and he breathed
his last on the field where he lay.   This unlooked-for
disaster spread such consternation among the Spanish
troops, that, had the rebels taken the advantage they
might have done at the sudden shock, almost amounting to a panic, which seized their opponents, they
might, at least in the first hours of confusion, have
gained some immediate if not permanent success. It is
doubtful, however, whether they knew what had really
occurred, until some time after; but it is certain that,
instead of advancing or even holding the ground they
possessed, they made a precipitate and somewhat
disorderly retreat, but were unpursued; so that this
eventful day of the seventeenth of August, which at
its commencement was supposed to herald something

decisive on one side or the other, left matters on the contrary much as they were, the loss of the unfortunate General Ena only excepted. The intelligence of his death caused universal regret in Havana, where he was respected in his public and loved in his private character. The highest honours were paid to his remains on their reaching Havana, whence they were conveyed on board ship, and carried to his native land for interment. Yet a few more days, and the last hopes of the invaders were destroyed, and the star of Lopez set for ever. The second in command after General Ena, Colonel Elizalde, came up with them at a place called Candillaria, and a sharp engagement took place, when they were totally routed. There now remained but a hundred followers of Lopez out of the number he had brought into this disastrous undertaking, and these few were in their turn encountered on the 24th, dispersed and scattered far and wide. And now began, for these unfortunate victims of the criminal ambition of Lopez, a series of hardships and miseries, the recital of which would seem rather to belong to the pages of a romance, than to be mere matter of actual fact. For many a long day and weary night did the wretched remnant of the invaders wander in the defiles, the woods, and the wilds of this unknown and to them inhospitable land, seeking shelter in caves, in holes, in trunks of old trees; without food,

I

almost without covering; that which they originally wore having been torn from their bodies
by the tangled thorns of the creepers and parasites
through which they had to make their way in their
precipitate flight; their flesh, too, torn and bleeding
from the rude contact of the prickly-pear abounding
throughout the Cordillera; forced to satisfy the
craving of hunger by eating the berries and even
leaves of trees; in danger from reptiles and their
poisonous bites; and, finally, tracked surely, if slowly,
by the far-famed Cuba bloodhounds. Their state
was indeed lamentable. How often did they bewail
the day they yielded to temptation! As may be
readily supposed, many of the young and tenderly-
reared among them sunk and died under these
accumulated sufferings and privations. Of the 500
who made good their landing, about 170 escaped
with life and were gradually caught, secured, and
imprisoned in Havana. Here they remained some
time, and were at least fed, clothed, and their wounds
tended. It might have been better, as things turned
out after all, if they had in the first instance given
themselves to the authorities, and trusted to their
clemency; but as they all lay under sentence of
death when caught, a proclamation to that effect
having been issued the day after the landing of the
expedition, they probably and naturally supposed,
after such repeated provocations, that no quarter

would be given them. The terrible misery they had undergone, however, added to their youth, and the obvious deceit of which they had been victims, were considered as sufficient expiation for their misdeeds. The pain of death was remitted; and, after a communication of the circumstances to the government in the mother-country, Queen Isabel granted them a free pardon, and they were shortly after permitted to return to the United States, cured for life, it is to be hoped, of filibusterism. . . .

CHAPTER XXXI.

IT only remains now on this subject to recount the fate of Lopez ; though this, being one of the salient points in the history of the troubles attending Spain at this period, is tolerably well known. After his final defeat on the 24th of August, he, with seven only of his companions, fled to the fastnesses in the vicinity of the Vuelta Abajo. Four experienced bloodhounds were placed on his track, aided by some soldiers to follow them. The glory of capturing him fell to the lot of a volunteer after all — a farmer, I believe, of the name of Castañeda. The bloodhounds had traced him to a gorge in the rocks of Rosario, where his human pursuers came up with him. He was secured, and brought into Havana by his captor, Castañeda. Small space was allowed him for any of this world's affairs. Since 1848, sentence of death had been hanging over him ; but had he been taken *then*, it is supposed he would at least have met with a soldier's doom, and been shot ; but, as it was, he was condemned to die the death of a felon: and so, on the third day after his capture, on the 1st of September, he was garotted on the Esplanade by the Morro.   A shocking sounding and still more shocking looking mode of execution (judging from the instrument, which I have seen), yet it is far more instantaneous in its effect than our fashion of hanging.   And so ended the eventful career of Lopez, and ends my narration of it, which has extended itself to a somewhat greater length than I anticipated when I began writing it.   Though necessarily imperfect in some of its details, from the time which has elapsed since these events took place, besides not having been on the spot then to hear them commented on as they occurred, I may at least hope to establish a claim to one merit in my relation, namely, truth.   The preceding account has been gathered from men of different opinions, and who consequently looked upon these occurrences from different points of view; yet all have in the aggregate agreed, not only as to the facts, but with little exception as to the guiding causes of the actions which took place.   Much I have learned from the Captain-General; and this might be deemed, therefore, by those unacquainted with General Cañedo's punctilious sense of honour, a one-sided statement; yet to all who have had the opportunity of knowing him, I need say nothing further in corroboration of the truth of any words uttered by him; and to those

who have not known him, I say merely, ask those
who have.   Another person to whom I am indebted
for much valuable and reliable information concerning the events which marked those days of agitation,
is a countryman of my own, Mr. Sidney Smith.
This gentleman, at the time of Lopez's invasion, was
secretary to the English Consulate at Havana, and
was what I call *on the other side;* that is, his com-
passion and sympathies were aroused on behalf of
the Americans : I do not mean in the first instance
of their invasion, but after the catastrophe had occurred, and the sun which had risen so brightly in
Bahia Honda had set in the prison of Havana.   He
then did all that mortal man could do to alleviate
their sufferings, and to soften the hardships of their
confinement.   Indeed, I am afraid his kind heart
would have prompted him even to endeavour to save .
Lopez himself from the garotting he so richly deserved.   At any rate, Mr. Smith devoted himself
entirely to these poor prisoners.   He gave them
money to procure better food for the sick and ailing;
he gave them sympathy; and, better than all, he
gave them his time.   He wrote to their parents and
friends to tell them all that might be told; and
many a mother's heart he gladdened by letting her
know that her child was at least in life.   Finally,
by his unwearying patience and indefatigable exer-
tions, he succeeded; and I do not think I am saying

too much when I attribute to his indomitable and
persevering efforts (at least to a very considerable
extent), the ultimate pardon and freedom granted
to the remnant of the band. The people in the
United States who were connected with and concerned in these affairs, I know, share this opinion ;
àpropos of which, before finally taking leave of this
subject, I must do the Americans the justice to say
that they have neglected no opportunity of testifying
their gratitude and appreciation of Mr. Sidney
Smith's generous and kind-hearted actions regarding
their unhappy countrymen. His first visit to the
States, after the events to which I have alluded, was
a perfect ovation from the beginning to the end of
his journey. In conclusion, it must seem even to
the most sanguine on the subject of the annexation
of Cuba by America, that whatever may be reserved
for the future to bring to pass, it is a futile and
utterly hopeless dream to indulge in at present.
Without going into the political question between
America and Spain, or the foreign influence in
Europe which would be brought to bear on the
subject upon either side, it seems clearly demon-
strated that Cuba herself wishes no change, and is
intrinsically loyal to the Spanish government. Were
this not the case, were the people disposed to foster
the growth of disaffection or rebellion, civil war
would ere now be rife throughout the island, and

when quelled in one spot would speedily break out in another. As I have had occasion to remark in the course of this little narrative, nature has provided every convenience, every facility, for resisting the powers that be. A very small number of rebels could hold out against an army, if they possessed the good-will of the peasants; but that up to the present time has ever failed invaders, — filibusteros pirates, *et hoc genus omne.* This is a voluminous letter, but I shall send it by a private hand.

Ever your affectionate,

C.

CHAPTER XXXII.

✻ *Havana, Nov.* 20*th.*—My dear Father,—Our time has passed very agreeably since our return from Mexico, chiefly in mixing with the private society, as there has been a good deal of party-giving during the last week or two. The hosts and hostesses here are every thing that can be wished for, and in this commendation I include those of all nations. Indeed it would be difficult to specify whether Spanish, English, French, German, or American have received us with the most cordiality and kindness. Mrs. Crawford, the wife of the English Consul, gives weekly receptions, or *tertullias où l'on s'amuse,* I must confess, far more than in our native "at homes" or *thé dansants.* I cannot help thinking that one cause of this is, that in England we all, not only the "budding misses," but all of us, more or less, are constantly thinking "what he, she, it, or they may be about." We are always wishing, hoping, or expecting *something*, and, until that something comes or happens, we make it a sort of point of honour to exemplify in another sense the

Irishman's exclamation, "I *will* not be pleased, and no one *shall* please me," instead of taking things as they come, or as they are, and making the most of them. We have spent also many pleasant days and evenings with two of the married sisters of Mrs. Crawford, who are married to Germans, and who reside outside the town, that is, in the Serro. The charm of these quintas is indescribable; the freshness of the air, and the fragrance of the shrubs and flowers, are perfectly delicious; and if, as sometimes occurred, we went at night, it reminded one of a fairy tale. We were literally lit " by the firefly's lamp," myriads of these beautiful little earthly stars attending us on our way. One English and two French men-of-war are here now, whose officers help to enliven our tertullias. We went last night to the Tacon with the Captain General, a grand gala night in honour of Queen Isabel's fête-day. The house was brilliantly illuminated *a giorno,* and above our box were suspended, for this occasion only, full length portraits of the Royal lady and her husband. Saw Matilda Diaz, a star of Old Spain, who has come to astonish the Havanese. But she had been ill, and her voice was still weak, so no doubt we heard her to disadvantage. The national air of Spain was played and sung as soon as the Captain-General entered the house. I like it very much. It is in march time, consequently quicker than ours, but very inspiring. I should mention that, before the opera yesterday, we were taken by the good nature of the Captain-General for a drive " in state," which was very amusing, as well as agreeable. Every body and every animal was dressed in full costume, something like our birthday drawing-room day in England. The carriage we were in was an open barouche, the arms of Spain emblazoned on the panels. The interior seats and cushions were of rich amber colour satin, and the horse's harness, caparisons, trappings, &c. all gold.

We took an early ride on horseback this morning to the village of Marianao a few miles out of town, and famous for the beauty of its scenery ; the multitude and grandeur of the

> —— " palms which never die, but stand
> Immortal sea marks on the strand,
> Their feathery tufts like plumage rare,
> Their stems so high, so strange, and fair; "

and, lastly, for a most picturesque and beautifully constructed bridge over the little river, Almendares, which is in fact the main object "to be admired," say the guide books, by the various people who make this excursion from Havana. It (the bridge) appeared to me to be very much on the principle of providing a cathedral arch for a goose to walk under, the river, or rather stream, appearing so completely out of all proportion to the magnificence of the bridge thrown

across it. Rivers and streams, however, in these parts
of the world, are not always so quiet as they look, and
no doubt there are sufficient reasons to justify the
strength given to this very handsome structure.
Marianao itself is a favourite resort for the townspeople, when they want a little repose or change of
air, which here is very pure and healthy; and the
town being built on the top of a hill, the climate is
considered more bracing than Havana; besides
being more à *la portée* of most people than the expensive semi-palaces of the " Serro," where the rich
merchants and noblesse chiefly go for their villeg-
giatura. On returning to Havana this morning, we
arrived at the city gates in company with all the
donkeys, mules, horses, and carts, with their respective
burdens, going to market : a busy as well as amusing scene. The sellers of vegetables and fruits especially, with their extraordinary yet musical cries;
the panniers laden with the weight of pine-
apples, melons, guavas bananas, oranges, lemons,
sapotes, cocoa-nuts, prickly pears, and several other
fruits of which I cannot tell the names, heaped together in luxuriant profusion : then the sellers of
fish with a still more motley and incomprehensible
collection ; the dealers in " aves," i. e., not " Ave-
Marias ! " but birds of all kinds, alive and dead.
This united collection of curiosities, both animal and
vegetable, formed altogether a scene I should think

unique of its kind. Seeing the various provisions,
too, in this manner, was more agreeable than paying
a visit to the market-place itself; as, in consequence
of the very dense assemblage of blacks in attendance
for the purpose of purveying for their own or their
master's household, the odours are not exactly those
of Araby the Blest.

24th. — The day after the rejoicings in honour of
the queen I have related in the earlier part of this
letter, a very tragical event has occurred. Madame
Domingue, the prima donna of the opera, a good
singer and a very pretty woman, was murdered by
her husband, on her return from the opera, where she
had been performing one of her favourite parts. She
was stabbed in forty different places. The wretched
man endeavoured to kill himself immediately afterwards but was unsuccessful; he has therefore been
brought to trial, and to-day was pronounced guilty.
Jealousy, as may be supposed, was the cause of the
crime. His hallucination on this point appears to
have been carried to such an extent, that I doubt
whether, had he been tried for the murder in England
instead of here, he would not have been acquitted on
the ground of insanity. He seems to have been
possessed with the idea that his wife was unfaithful
to him, and that the object of her fancy was the
Captain-General! Moreover he persuaded himself
that she was in the habit of getting up from her bed

in the middle of the night for the purpose of visiting her supposed lover at the Quinta! As all this was manifestly a delusion, she having been actually present before his eyes on some of the occasions he maintained she was absent, besides it being proved that the Captain-General had never seen Madame Domingue at all, except on the stage, it would seem certain that the unfortunate man was not a responsible being. Still, I am very much inclined to think it more merciful to society in general to put an end to so dangerous a lunatic as this. Mad or not, when one person deliberately cuts another to pieces, he may well meet the fate of an assassin. The authorities here are apparently of the same opinion, as this malefactor is condemned to the garotte, and will be executed in a few days. . . . We are going to-morrow a few miles into the country for the purpose of visiting a tobacco plantation. I shall write an account of it in my next. For the present, then, adieu.

Ever your affectionate,

C.

CHAPTER XXXIII.

Havana, November 26th. — My dear Father, — We have now returned from the proposed visit to a "Vega" or tobacco plantation, to which I alluded in my last letter, and we have greatly enjoyed our excursion. I was anxious to see, and if possible to thoroughly understand, all about this very important branch belonging to the "Cosas de Cuba." This ground of which I am now writing is on an estate belonging to Queen Christina of Spain, who possesses a good bit of property of one kind or another in this island. A very important accessory to all lots or portions of land devoted to the culture of the tobacco-plant is a river, or running stream, in the close vicinity. Whether this be an indispensable adjunct or not I could not clearly discover, but the intendente who explained everything to me said the cigarros were always much finer flavoured when grown near water; and certainly, as far as I can recollect, in all the tobacco grounds I have seen there was always a rivulet at least of some kind or another close by. The proper name, by the way, of what we

call tobacco; is " Cohiba," but in the olden time, when
the Spaniards first came across the Atlantic, among
other good will offerings made them by the Indians
were "tobaccos" of the cohiba plant; that is to
say, the rolled leaf or leaves (cigars in short) prepared
for smoking was named by them a " tobacco ;" hence
the mistake arose, the Spanish supposing the name of
the manufacture was the name of the plant.   This
error has, however, never yet been corrected, and is not
likely to be so, now that long use and habit have
sanctioned the wrong appellation.   To proceed therefore, *tobacco* (not cohiba) is seldom grown in larger
lots or portions of ground than would cover about
twenty acres in one place.   I mean by this, that one
proprietor may possess three or four, or more tobacco
gardens or plantations, but they are studded about
different parts of his territory, and no one of them
is of greater extent than from twenty to thirty acres.
The principal reason of these small subdivisions is,
that, being a tolerably manageable article of culture,
small capitalists may venture on it ; consequently, in
many and most instances, the grounds are underlet,
and rented of the original proprietor.   Another
and very important circumstance in favour of culti-
vating tobacco in preference to other natural productions here, especially for the majority of European
residents, is that it can be tended by white people.
From six to eighteen or twenty labourers, according

to the size of the lot, are sufficient for all that is required in the management. Before the year 1820, tobacco was a government monopoly, but since then this restriction has been removed with respect to *Cuba*, a tax only being levied on each arroba or weight of 25 lbs. In Old Spain, I believe, the monopoly still exists on all grown in the country actually. But it was found not to answer in the colonies. My cicerone, who was good-natured enough not only to explain in an ordinary way, but to tell me all the various processes and stages from the very beginning, said there was little manual labour or difficulty in its cultivation, but that it required the most constant watching and care, and, furthermore, no little exercise of judgment as to the proper times and seasons in which to cut, to prune, to clip, to water, and to thin in quantity, so very much of the after goodness and delicacy of flavour, whether in cigars or in snuff, depending on their treatment in this their infant cabbage state; and this knowledge cannot be gained by the laying down of regular rules, or any distinct course of treatment, but must be the result of careful observation and repeated experiences. When the season of gathering arrives, the leaves are stripped from the stem, spread out as flat as may be, and placed in packets of twos and threes to dry. These leaves have been divided into four different classes, each varying in its degree of excellence. Speaking of the tobacco plant as of a cabbage,— to which it bears more resemblance than any other I can think of,— the leaves nearest the heart are the most valuable, and are called "desechos." Those immediately contiguous to them come next; they are named " desechitos." The two remaining qualities, numbers three and four, are respectively called "libras " and "injuriados." They are formed of the lower and coarser leaves of the plant; the "libras" being the better and tenderer, and the "injuriados " being the lower and external leaves nearest to the root and the ground. This last class, namely, the injuriados, are in their turn sub-divided into three; called "injuriado de *repaso*" (which means chosen or selected), "injuriados *primeras*," and "*segundas*." There is, in addition to those I have mentioned, another hybrid sort, composed of the slightly injured leaves of classes *two* and *three*, namely, the desechitos and libras, which go by the rather contradictory name of "injuriados buenos." And indeed I may add another and worst class, made of worm-eaten or otherwise spoilt leaves. This is uncompromisingly and frankly called here " injuriado malo; but I am by no means sure that it is not sold in other countries under a far better sounding name. Having given these details so far, I will now return to the *packets* on the drying-ground before mentioned. When sufficiently dried, they are collected together

and assorted in bundles, rather resembling sheaves
of corn; each sheaf containing about fifty leaves of
number four, or injuriados, and twenty-five leaves
of number three, or libras.   These sheaves are in
their turn formed into larger loads, at the rate of
four to a faggot, and are then called " manojos." A
hundred and forty manojos constitute a "tercio;"
and it is in this form they are sent away from their
native earth, either to be rolled into cigars or used
à la Yankee, &c.   Two tercios constitute a weight,
called a carga, equal to eight arrobas, or 200 lbs.
This measure is the one which is charged for — so
much a carga — in questions of freight.   Connected
with these manojos, I observed a curious purpose to
which the bark of the palm tree is put.   The outer
peel of the stem, which is of a kind of scaly sub-
stance, being removed, it is used as an envelope or
covering for each tercio, or bundle of 140 manojos,
preserving the tobàcco hermetically from air, damp,
or other injury.   These envelopes are called in Cuban
dialect, " yaguas."   From the above particulars,
which I hope I have given with sufficient clearness
to be useful to those who may be interested in the
subject, it will be seen that the first or ultra-superior
sort of cigars must necessarily be small in quantity
compared to those made from the more numerous
and larger leaves.   Still it may be satisfactory to
know, if you cannot get the best, what the next

qualities should be, and also what are good mixtures. The proportionate produce of the various qualities, according to the returns of the year 1853, was, to a "caballeria" or piece of ground of thirty-two acres, 9,000 lbs. of tobacco. Of this quantity, 450 lbs. only (or one-twentieth) are contributed by the desechos, or first class; 1800 by the desechitos; 2250 by the libras; and 4500 by the injuriados. In speaking of the various sorts, it may be remembered that I have mentioned some of the leaves as worm-eaten. On this part of the history of tobacco culture my guide was most eloquent. It would appear that a taste for "the fragrant weed" is by no means confined to the human race: every description of worm, snail, and creeping thing seems to be addicted to the habit. Month after month do their depredations continue, and one marauder only gives way to be succeeded by another worse than himself. It is the injury and often destruction caused by these insects that renders it imperative on the tobacco-grower to keep such a continual watch over his plants, to examine them narrowly, and every day, and to be on the look-out to discover and arrest, before it be too late, the inroads of the enemy. By far the most formidable of these insect adversaries, however, is the ant; and of this tribe a particular species, called "vivijaguas," are blessed with so voracious an appetite, that woe be to the unlucky plantation into

which they succeed in making good their entry.
It is but rarely they can be expelled before they
have devoured everything. I was told — but the
relation seems to me so apocryphal, that in re-
peating it I merely "tell the tale as told to me,"
not as believing it, namely — that the plague of ants,
having at one time reached such a degree of intensity, that the whole tobacco trade was threatened with annihilation, when some inventive genius
bethought him of *importing* a foreign army for the
purpose of exterminating the natives! *France* was
applied to (I should have thought America more to
the purpose), who benevolently furnished a "legion"
of ants, which speedily commenced operations, and
by keeping the unfortunate aborigines in constant
hot water by means of skirmishes, sieges, and battles,
saved the tobacco crops! In addition to these
terrestrial helps, the powers above come in also for
their share of praise and gratitude. A celestial
worthy called Saint Marcial, and whose prowess and
exploits against *ants* seem to have beaten Saint
George and the dragon quite to smithereens, has
masses and all manner of similar delicate attentions
paid to him by the tobacco-growing portion of the
inhabitants of the beautiful "Queen of the Antilles."
His day is the 30th of June, on which occasion all
tobacco-growers here go to church, even if the ants
keep them away on other occasions. In conclusion

of " the great tobacco question," it may be mentioned that the quantity now exported annually from Cuba averages 11,250,000 lbs. of branch or leaf tobacco, and 1,250,000 lbs. twisted rolls or cigars (I speak now of *legal* exportation); and the quantity consumed in the island averages about 7,500,000, but an immense deal it is well known is smuggled in spite of the vigilance of the authorities. The parts of Cuba most favourable to the growth and good condition of the plant are the western and southern districts generally. In the east the produce is of an inferior kind. The sort called " Virginian " is chiefly grown here. The proprietor or renter of a vega does not depend, however, only on tobacco for his livelihood or profit. By a bountiful provision of nature, the same soil is peculiarly propitious to the constitution of the plantain tree, which may almost be termed the bread and meat of the labourer in the tropics; they roast, fry, boil, and dress the fruit in every imaginable way, and can by the addition sometimes of a little rice, or chilis, or oil, or frijoles (a sort of red bean greatly liked), vary their food or its mode of preparation every day. In all vegas therefore the plantain tree holds a distinguished situation; besides, though that is of no consequence to the agriculturist, the general character of the ground is infinitely improved in a picturesque point of view by the intermixture of these graceful trees with the cabbagy-looking tobacco bushes. It is calculated that the number of plantains, that is to say, the fruit produced by the plantain tree, exceeds that of all the other vegetable productions of the same class* added together. The government, who institute the most minute statistical inquiries concerning everything, have obtained on this head, for instance, the curious computation that ten millions four hundred thousand arrobas, which multiplied by twenty-five make two hundred and sixty millions lbs. weight of plantains, are annually grown in Cuba.

* Namely, the Yuca or Cassava root, the Baniato, the Ñame, and Malanga, the three last being species of potatoes and yams.

CHAPTER XXXIV.

THE Captain-General has sent me a beautiful present in the shape of a genuine Havana fan. The carvings in mother-of-pearl and tortoiseshell, executed by the Havanese artisans, are extraordinary specimens of fine and curious workmanship, fan-making being the principal and most lucrative branch of their handiwork. I do not know, and do not remember whether any ancient chroniclers inform us, if fans were used in Spain before the discovery of America, though, judging by the manners and customs of the people here, I should be rather inclined to think this must have been their native place. During the whole time of my sojourn in Cuba, I never remember a single instance of noticing a native woman or girl without a fan in her hands. Of course they vary much in quality, but of some kind or other, a fan is an indispensable adjunct to the get-up of the female sex. That which I have just received is most elaborately and delicately carved in mother-of-pearl. The intricacies of a design embracing fruit, flowers,

and birds, are worked with the most wonderful
minuteness; indeed, so much so as to more resemble
those curious and skilfully cut-out papers one sees
placed over French plums or bonbons. The tips of
these finely worked, expensive fans are, like this one,
painted either on parchment or vellum, and are im-
ported from Paris, painting being one of the fine
arts in which the Cubans have yet to distinguish
themselves. Tortoiseshell, as I have also mentioned,
is brought to as great a state of perfection in the
carving as mother-of-pearl. While on the subject
of hand labour I must not omit to notice another
manufacture for which one part of the island, the
coast near and about Trinidad, is famous, namely, the
making sticks, canes, and various similar kinds of
objects, of the bones of a colossal fish, called the
" manati," or sea-cow. The manati chiefly resorts to
the mouths of rivers, and shows a preference for
what is neither quite salt nor quite fresh water. In
appearance it greatly resembles a whale, but with
rather a pig-shaped head. I can only judge, however, from pictures, as I never was lucky enough to
see one either alive or dead. The back-bone is the
part most generally used for the articles they manufacture from the animal, as the purest and clearest
pieces are here obtained. The cane is of most
remarkable strength, and has the colour and apparent consistency of amber, but is far harder and

K

stronger.   So great indeed is considered to be the
danger which might accrue from either a thoughtless
or angry use of it, that its employment as a walking-
stick or weapon is absolutely prohibited in the island,
a very slight stroke having been attended some time
since with fatal results.   Nevertheless, it seems to me
to be a most arbitrary and moreover useless measure
to forbid their use, as a death-blow might be dealt
with any sort of stick if maliciously and violently
struck.   I should for my part, however, even were
there no prohibition, think their weight in the hand
the most forcible argument, especially in a hot climate, against carrying them about.   Even when,
only of the thickness of most ordinary sticks, they are
most unpleasantly heavy.

November 30*th.*—Went to the opera to-night for
the double purpose of thanking the Captain-General
for the fan, and also to try my hand at flirting it in
the proper Havanese manner.   I think I have succeeded pretty well, and shall no doubt improve with
practice.   The only difficulty is to flirt it slowly
enough, so as to give the long, drawling kind of rattle
which is so marked a peculiarity to be observed in
the Tacon assemblages.   A drawling rattle seems a
contradictory form of expression, yet I can think of
no better term to describe my meaning.   All the
fans, with very few exceptions, being made, as I have
before said, of mother-of-pearl or tortoiseshell, the

sort of clicking sound of the opening and closing one
fan in the orthodox slow and measured way, when
multiplied four or five hundred times and continued
incessantly, gives very much this impression to the
ear. Yet, strange to say, the effect is by no means
disagreeable. Though a noise certainly, it is a gentle
one, and actually harmonises very well with the
music. Apropos of national customs, it is a singular
fact that the graceful and beautiful Spanish mantilla does not find favour with the fair inhabitants
of Cuba. It is the more incomprehensible that
whereas in Mexico, where the Spaniards no longer
rule, the fashion of wearing mantillas among the
higher, and rebosos (a coarser sort of the same thing)
among the lower classes, still universally prevails ;
here, on the contrary, though essentially Spanish in
other tastes and opinions, a mantilla is never seen.
Women, old and young, drive about in their *volantes*
with *decolletées* dresses of all colours, the señoras
blazing with jewels on both neck and head, and the
señoritas with wreaths or bunches of flowers. Also I
must not forget a most important item in Havana
toilettes, namely, the cascarilla powder which they
all, but more especially the young, most plentifully lay on their faces, necks, arms, and hands. It
is used in the most incredible quantities, but without
the slightest attempt at disguise: indeed, they say,
and no doubt with truth, that it saves them from

K 2

being burnt by sun or wind. But the effect, especially at night, is singular in the extreme. One does
not always *see* the powder then (indeed, one can very
seldom distinguish it by candle-light), and as they
never use rouge, the contrast between their magnificent black hair, large dark eyes, and the snowy
appearance given to the skin by this powder, affords
a most striking *coup d'œil* — particularly remarkable when they are dancing at a ball or tertullia — no
heat, no exercise, ever causing any apparent alteration
in the complexion, or sending any visible flush to
the cheek. In speaking of the Havanese manner of
spending the evening, their music or their dancing,
as the case may be, I should not omit mentioning a
nightly custom, not the least singular or romantic of
the catalogue, — I mean the musical cries of the watch-
men calling the hours of the night. To me it is quite
an inducement to try and remain awake for two or
three hours for the purpose of listening to them. They
generally begin by some kind of invocation to the
Virgin, coupled with the name occasionally of the
saint whose day it may happen to be. For example,
" Ave Maria sanctissima! Madre de Dios! y Santa
Teresa Virgen! Estan las dos de la manaña y sereno."
As it is very seldom that the weather is anything
else than " sereno," there is little variation in the
latter part of this oration; but the tone, the melody,
is really beautiful. The whole is sung like an opera

" recitative," and the last word " sereno " is cadenced
with a " sweetness long drawn out," reminding one
of Mario's " Addio ! " I must now conclude this
longish letter. I fear the tobacco part of it will not
interest you greatly, not being a smoker. Still, as
tobacco is so very important a matter in Cuba, I
have given you a little sketch on the subject.

Your always affectionate,

C.

CHAPTER XXXV.

Havana, Dec. 2nd. — The time is now rapidly approaching, my dear Father, when we must take a long farewell, I fear, of Havana, as I have promised to spend Christmas-day at Barbados. Yesterday our old friend, Captain Parker, commanding the "Dee," arrived here on his way to Vera Cruz. He was detained at New York a considerable time, the work-people there having had a great press of business on hand. However, the old ship looks considerably the better for the painting and decoration she has received. We have decided on going to St. Thomas in her when she returns from the Vera Cruz trip. This Captain Parker expects to be in about a fortnight. Meantime we shall endeavour to visit some other parts of this island, although it will be difficult to tear ourselves away from the pleasant daily routine of our lives at Havana.

Dec. 5th. — The Fates have been unpropitious; for after having all in readiness to set out on our little tour Tuesday last, the illness of the friend who was

to accompany us has delayed us till now, and now
our time is short. To save as much as possible we
went last night by steamboat to Matanzas, which we
reached this morning (the 6th) after a rougher and
more unpleasant passage than we have yet experienced
since we first ventured on the Atlantic. Every one
was ill, myself included, wonderful to relate — very dis-
creditable, I must confess, for a twelve hours' voyage!
We brought with us a letter of introduction to Mr.
Brinckenhoff, a gentleman residing here (a partner
in the banking-house of Drake & Co.). This gentleman has most kindly placed everything at our " disposition," and among other things has provided us
with saddle-horses. So when it had become rather
cooler we set out, and had a most delightful ride in
view of one of the most beautiful and thoroughly
tropical scenes we have yet witnessed in our wanderings. Cumbre and the valley of " Yumuri " were the
two points of destination in our excursion. The
word " Yumuri " has a romantic and mournful derivation. In ancient days, soon after the discovery of the
western world, the original inhabitants of this valley were cruelly persecuted by the Spaniards in their
fanatic zeal for the spread of Christianity. After being
hunted like wild beasts from place to place, bloodhounds were finally employed to track them. In the
desperation they were driven to, sooner than be mas-
sacred in cold blood, many of them threw themselves

from the heights into the river flowing below, with the wailing cry of " *Yo moir !* " " I die : " hence the name *Yumuri.* It was very lovely, and reminded me of the far-famed description of the Vale of Cashmere. We looked down from a great height over groves of palm-trees (the trees of fairy-land), orange trees bending beneath their burden of golden fruit, sugar plantations spreading far and wide, over hill and dale, all tinged with a colour the tropics alone can show; then the winding river, and the bright sparkling blue sea in the distance bounding all, formed a picture not easily to be forgotten.

7th.—Set out very early this morning by the "Coliseo" railroad, and in about an hour stopped at Cardenas, near which place is the residence of a planter to whose house we were addressed by Mr. Brinckenhoff. They are Americans, and gave us a kindly and hospitable welcome and an excellent breakfast, after which we mounted our horses, and this time took a longer ride than before. After a course of ten miles, we reached a sugar estate belonging to Mr. Drake, and christened by the American name of Saratoga. He (Mr. Drake) is now in Paris, but has left his slaves and estate in the care of a superintendent who received us. We went to the sugar-house, and saw the whole process of making the sugar. Everything now is rendered comparatively easy to the slaves here, owing to the use of machinery. Perhaps the

most interesting part of the whole is the first
process which the sugar-canes undergo when cut
from the plantation or field. They are sent pell-
mell into a machine looking like a tilted waggon,
by which they are impelled down an inclined plane,
and when they reach the bottom they are caught
in the embrace of two huge rollers turned by a
steam engine, and by them are crushed and ground
into shapeless pulps. The pure syrup thus produced
is the " first state " of the sugar. The slaves, *malgré*
Mrs. Beecher Stowe, look exceedingly happy, and
*un*interesting. Mr. Drake has about 600 on this
estate. After having nearly boiled ourselves in the
sugar-house, we mounted our horses and rode all
round the estate and through the plantations. I
never enjoyed a ride so much, nor experienced such
complete novelty. Far as the eye could reach,
the sugar-canes spread themselves around us, looking
at a distance like a vast jungle, — monotonous, yet
possessing a beauty peculiarly their own, with the
tender green of their tapering leaves, and undeni-
able grace of their feathery flowers crowning the
canes as with delicate blue plumes. Then the exhi-
larating effect on the spirits of cantering over the
soft turf through the long glades cut in every direction though the canes. I should never have tired
for my own part, I believe, but my steed demanded
some consideration; so, most reluctantly, I wended

my way at length back to the house. We paid another visit at night to the sugar-buildings. Saw the slaves at supper, and tasted some capital bread and treacle they offered us.

8th. — Returned to Matanzas very much gratified by all we had seen. Mr. Brinckenhoff having kindly pressed us to stay another day with him and his daughter, we have, nothing loth, accepted his good-natured invitation. After breakfast we took a walk about the town, and along the sea-shore for some distance; a pretty, bright scene, and most agreeable temperature. In the afternoon we visited Mr. B.'s tobacco ground.

9th.—After having passed a most agreeable time with our kind hosts at Matanzas, we this morning returned by the Guines railroad though Regla to Havana. Here we found our old friend the Captain-General making his preparations for departure, his three years of government having nearly expired. He and his suite are to start on their return to Spain the week after we leave. Sorry as I am to bid farewell to Havana on many accounts, it is some small consolation that one of the best and most valued of our friends here is going away too. He has made me a present of two dear little gazelles, which I shall hope to be able to keep alive in England; also three very handsome specimens of Labrador ducks, with which I propose ornamenting the Chauntry ponds. General Cañedo had a small menagerie at his quinta, being particularly fond of animals. These gazelles were his especial pets: it is therefore doubly kind of him to give them to me. Captain Parker has most good-naturedly offered to take charge of them, see they are well lodged and fed on board ship, and bring them safe to England.*

As we shall be very busy from now until the time of our departure, I shall close this letter. If I have time I will write once again before leaving.

Ever your affectionate,

C.

---

* My hopes on this subject were never realised. Spite of every care, the poor gazelles died within a week of leaving the tropics. A bitter east wind in the English Channel finished them.

CHAPTER XXXVI.

Havana, December 26th. — My dear Father, — The "Dee" arrived to-day, and if all be well we shall hope to embark in her to-morrow; but the last of our sojourn here has been saddened by a most unexpected and melancholy occurrence. Two days after my last letter, a young man of about two-and-twenty, the nephew of a gentleman (a judge by profession, I understand) who had only arrived from New Orleans a few days previously, complained in the middle of dinner that he felt ill. He was recommended to go to bed and take some simple remedy, it being supposed he had got a chill which a night's rest would cure. Nothing more was then thought of the incident, and if any anxiety were expressed it was rather for the uncle, who was an old man, I believe, but I never saw him, and who had never come out of his room since his arrival at the hotel. The next day the young man was pronounced better, and was to get up and join us at table at supper. He did not come, however, but about twelve o'clock at night, I,

whose bedroom was next to his, was aroused by hearing moans and the sound of some one tossing about
violently in bed.   I immediately woke up the mistress of the hotel and the servants, and the doctor
being summoned instantly, the disease was declared
to be yellow fever in its worst form.   But this, terrible as it was, was not so bad as what followed.   The
surprise and the sudden shock, I suppose, of the much
dreaded "vomito" being so near in all its horrors,
caused such a panic among the inmates of the house
that the morning had scarcely dawned before they all
took their departure, and I am sorry to add that of
many American women who were under this roof not
one remained to help their countryman in his hour
of need.   The whole affair seems to me like a
frightful dream.   Towards the end of the day, partly
from curiosity and partly from solicitude, and moreover not having the slightest fear of infection myself,
I went into the sufferer's room, and there witnessed
that which decided me to remain and tend him till
all should be over, whether for good or for evil.   A
nurse had been engaged — sent from the hospital —
a thorough hireling; and as I entered she was en-
deavouring violently to force a spoon with some ice
in it between the poor patient's teeth, which, in the
strong convulsive fits which at periods attacked him,
nearly locked the teeth together.   Poor fellow! he
was quite sensible then, though he could not speak.

I saw, by the wistful look of his eyes, how he appreciated gentle handling and speaking to. Some hours after, in an interval of calm, he told me he recognised me, and called me by my name. Another night and another day dragged on, when towards five o'clock it became evident the end was approaching. I think nearly at the last he was conscious, as he signed to me to take his hand and warm it between mine, as I had done before. He then turned his head away; and about half an hour after that, the doctor pronounced all was over — the pulse had ceased to beat.

Now that the reaction has come, and I have time to think, I begin both to feel frightened and to wonder if I shall escape, not only on my own account, but on E———'s, who was too courageous to run away like the rest. Still, though I did not go near her during this painful week, she was under the same roof. The Captain-General has just been spending one last hour with us to say good-bye, and in hopes we may all meet again in the old country. We are to embark at sunset, dull and dispirited enough; but we must hope for the best, though danger is not considered over for nine days.

Ever your affectionate,

C.

CHAPTER XXXVII.

St. Thomas, Dec. 21st. — My dear Father, — You will be glad to find by the date of this that we have arrived here in safety, and I am happy to add that the sea-breeze and change of scene have had a very beneficial effect; I am fast recovering from my depression, and hope I am no longer in danger of catching the fever. St. Thomas looks green and pretty as before, though now it has lost the charm of novelty. The weather being fine and calm, Captain Parker sent us in the boat on an excursion to San Martin, another of the little cluster of islands belonging to the Danish crown. San Martin is chiefly frequented as a kind of watering-place for the benefit of the residents in St. Thomas when they wish to " go out of town." The Governor is now here with his family. Our principal reason for making this marine promenade was to avoid being present at the disagreeable operation of coaling, which renders the vessel almost unbearable while it lasts, the black dust penetrating into every nook and

corner, however well guarded; besides which the
coal wharf is said to be the most unhealthy spot
possible—the hot-bed of yellow fever, cholera, and
all manner of diseases. They have a strange custom
here which I should not forget to mention, namely,
that the actual bodily labour of carrying the loads
of coals from their original depôt at the wharf to the
ship's side is performed by *women*, whose privilege
it especially is, and who would energetically resist
any encroachment by the other sex. We have just
returned from our expedition. The old "Dee" is in
tolerable order, but the world in general is in a great
state of dismay and tribulation. You would never
guess what has happened, so I must tell you. A
ship, laden with ice, from the United States has
struck upon one of the Virgin Gordoa rocks. The
crew are all safe and sound, but the ice has gone to
the bottom of the sea. It sounds rather ridiculous
to hear the lamentations raised in consequence of
this catastrophe; still, no doubt we as well as others
shall feel the discomfort of getting warm wine and
water, melted butter, &c. An odd complaint—is it
not?—to make at Christmas time!

Martinique, Dec. 24th.—Since leaving St. Thomas
three days ago we have been winding through the
mazes, and touching for a few hours at many of these
beautiful Windward Islands, or lesser Antilles. St.
Christopher's or St. Kitt's, Nevis, Montserrat, Anti-

gua, Dominica, and Guadaloupe were successively visited. The islands of St. Kitt's and Nevis are within sight of each other. The former, of which the principal town is called Basse Terre, is of a hilly, rugged character, but wondrously green. One of the eminences I particularly observed as resembling smooth green velvet, is called " Monkey Hill." These animals are to be found in abundance here. A mountain peak about 2000 feet above the sea bears the unpleasant name of Mount Misery. Moreover the fort and head-quarters of whatever regiment may happen to be stationed here is placed on one " Brimstone Hill." Disagreeable associations, I think, accompany both these names; yet, as far as I could judge in my short visit, there seemed nothing to justify any complaints either of the climate or fertility of the soil. Nevis is most remarkably beautiful. The island appears to be composed of one large mountain, rising from the sea to the sky until its crest is lost in the clouds. It is supposed that the present name of Nevis is a corruption from " Nieves," the Spanish for " snow," and that Columbus, who was its discoverer, called it " Nieves " from the white clouds hovering round its summit and giving it the appearance of being snow-capped. The vegetation is peculiarly luxuriant, the mountain side clothed with sugar-cane, while graceful groups of palmetto, fern, and cocoa-nut trees detach themselves in dark relief against the paler hue of the canes. The steamer anchored in the small bay of Charlestown, a little place scarcely more than a village in size, but which enjoys the honour of being called the capital of Nevis. Montserrat, with the singular-looking rock near it called Redonda, was next touched at, but here we did not land. A few hours after brought us to Antigua, where we anchored in what is called English Harbour. The general character of the scenery to be distinguished from this point is not at all un-English, no palms or other essentially tropical plants being visible, and the shore being rather flat. There are two small forts opposite to each other commanding the entrance to the harbour. These forts are respectively named Fort Charlotte and Fort Berkeley. I was in hopes of meeting with the Bishop of Antigua and Mrs. Davis, who came out with us in the " Paranà" from England, and who wished us to pay them a visit in the course of our peregrinations. But I heard that at present they are staying at St. John's, the cathedral town of Antigua, which is about twelve miles off, and consequently too far to enable us to go there and return before the " Conway" resumes her voyage. I hope, however, on our way back to be able to devote a day to them. We left Santa Maria de la Antigua, to call it by its real full-length designation, at dusk, and the next morning at seven o'clock found ourselves in the roadstead of the French island of Guadaloupe. Being very anxious to see both the colonies belonging to France in the Caribbean seas, or as much of them as was practicable, I took the opportunity of the first boat bound for the shore to place myself in her, and landed at Basse Terre. It is curious to observe how, in spite of difficulties or obstacles, natural or otherwise, the French always manage to give a sort of Parisian air to whatever town or place they may occupy. The first object which met my gaze on landing was something very much resembling a *boulevard*,—a long street going up a steepish hill to be sure, but with formal rows of trees at each side of the way. That the trees happened to be palms and mangoes was a little variety certainly, but there they were; there also were the gaily decorated shops, the cafés, the little marble tables and wooden-backed chairs. Basse Terre, moreover, seems in all respects a cheerful, flourishing, and very picturesque town. The houses are mostly painted in gay colours. This practice, when employed in a sunny climate and under a bright sky like this, greatly enhances the beauty of the outward appearance of ordinary habitations. The Place d'Armes, where a parade was taking place, struck me as very like that of Havana, only on a smaller scale. I lingered for some time watching the scene, enjoying the early morning air, and listen-

ing to the merry strains of the regimental band.
We now proceeded to ascend the heights behind the
town, not a very easy task, as those *boulevard* streets
whereof I have before made mention are not only
carried up the steepest of hills, but are paved with
those particularly disagreeable sharp-pointed stones
or pebbles which make one shrink at every step.
But in due time we were amply repaid by the magnificent prospect afforded us. The Souffrière, a
volcanic mountain of nearly 5000 feet, frowns over
the island and gives grandeur to the landscape,
while the numerous forests and groves of trees and
shrubs of every variety of hue, gently undulating
down to the calm blue sea, shed a charm over every
object; and even our *old tub,* i. e. the " Conway,"
looked well, or at least dignified, sleeping on the
quiet waters. The Souffrière keeps up a pretty
constant habit of smoking, and a few sparks are
occasionally to be seen; but no mention is made by
the inhabitants of Guadaloupe of anything like an
eruption. On descending to the town again we were
conducted into the house of one of the French
officials, I do not know who; but we were regaled with
a most excellent *déjeûner à la fourchette,* partly
French, partly West Indian cuisine; but most excellent and acceptable it was, hungry, thirsty, hot
and tired as we were. (Should I be fortunate enough
to number our hospitable Amphitryon amongst my

readers, I hope he will observe, that although a considerable time has elapsed, I have neither forgotten the incident nor his courtesy.) We now re-embarked, bade adieu to Guadaloupe, and towards the middle of the day made Dominica. The approach to this island showed finer scenery, I think, than any of those at which we have yet touched; stupendous precipices rise straight from the water's edge, but in the interstices and clefts of the ravines formed by them grows the most luxuriant vegetation. I do not ever remember having seen such beautiful ferns as are found here. Their variety seems endless. The town where the steamer calls to receive and take the mails is called Roseau. I believe there is a small stream in the neighbourhood which gives its name to the town, which, by the way, is rather difficult of access. There is no harbour, and you must land in boats across a surf which in any but the calmest weather is both disagreeable and dangerous. Roseau, and indeed, I believe, Dominica itself, are not either of them in a sufficiently flourishing condition to allow of the expenditure which would be necessary for the formation of a harbour, or the building of many other edifices which are now wanting. There is absolutely nothing worthy of remark in Roseau, the view and general aspect of the surrounding country being the only inducement to land. On the apparently flat summit of a

steep eminence called Morne Bruce, the little gar-
rison thought necessary for the preservation of
Dominica in the way it should go, or stop, is
quartered. It must be a dreary life for the soldiers
in spite of the beauty of the scenery. About eighteen
miles from here is Prince Rupert's Bay, also, I
believe, a very beautiful part of the island, but
which we had not time to visit. Here tradition
says that the gallant Prince Rupert died, and his tomb
is shown on the sea-shore.* Coffee seems to be the
most successful production of Dominica as far as
I can judge. We observed several healthy-looking
plantations, and were informed that the commerce
with the neighbouring islands, particularly the
French, in this commodity, forms a favourable contrast to other matters in general. Leaving Roseau,
a very short run now sufficed to bring us to Martinique, and we have just cast anchor in the Bay of
St. Pierre.

I fear we have been unwittingly the cause of
much disappointment to the good people here. As
we were preparing to get into the boat for the
purpose of going on shore, we were attracted by the
signs of an unusual stir on land, canopies being
erected, crimson carpets spread over the ground,

* This must be a popular error. Prince Rupert died in London,
but his brother, Prince Maurice, was drowned in these waters;
hence perhaps the mistake.

triumphal arches of shrubs and flowers raising themselves on high from places where they had evidently lain in readiness; and lastly, multitudes of people hastening to the water's edge all on the tiptoe of expectation of something or somebody. As we neared the shore and could distinguish the countenances, we observed looks of blank disappointment and surprise. The mystery was soon solved. A new archbishop has lately been appointed to the see of Martinique, and he was expected and ought to have come by this month's vessel, and all manner of honours and fêtes, as I have said, were awaiting him. But the ludicrous part of the affair was, that, whether from the distance of the ship or that the expectant multitude had no telescope, it appears that at first they mistook *me* and my friend for the bishop and chaplain, and only discovered their error when our proximity showed we were women! I imagine this absurd *quiproquo* must have arisen from the circumstance of our being both enveloped in black silk mantillas instead of bonnets, and these at a distance might have been mistaken for priests' garments. It was too late, however, to undo in a moment all that had been prepared; so over the carpets and under the arches we walked, and thus made our triumphal *entrée* into St. Pierre. I must do the St. Pierreians, however, the justice to say that notwithstanding their annoyance and their having so much trouble for nothing, they showed nothing but good-nature and the national good breeding towards us, helping us and giving us all necessary information to enable us to see as much of Martinique as we could during our short stay. The town of St. Pierre bears a great resemblance to its sister city in Guadaloupe, the same cheerful-looking cottages, the quays bordered with trees, and the streets have a similar *boulevard* look. Martinique has, I think, the advantage in general beauty of scenery. It is, in truth, "with verdure clad" of the loveliest hue. There appear to be more palm-trees here too than I have seen anywhere since leaving Cuba, and here they seem to grow up to the extreme top of the mountains, and, as may be supposed, much enhance the grandiose and majestic appearance of the land. This island has ever possessed great attraction in my eyes, from being the birth-place of Josephine, the cradle of her che-quered life.* After our departure from St. Pierre, and just as the day was declining, we came in sight of the "Diamond Rock," a sugarloaf-shaped hill at the extreme south of the island, and the scene in olden times of many hard struggles between us and France. There is a tale told of a naval hero (Captain

* Since these lines were written, a marble statue has been erected to the memory of the Empress Josephine by order of the present Emperor of the French.

Morris) having swung up a cannon to the top of the rock, and so caused wonderful deeds to be done to the detriment of the French; but it is a tale so oft told about no end of places in this part of the world, besides forming an incident in one of Captain Marryatt's "veracious" novels, that I am inclined to treat the whole affair as a fiction. So, with this apocryphal anecdote, I shall conclude my letter now, it. being nearly twelve o'clock, and I am going on deck to see the moon shining on St. Lucia.

Ever your affectionate,

C.

CHAPTER XXXVIII.

Barbados, Christmas night.—My dear Father,—
I have now reached the goal, and attained what, on
leaving England, was the only object of my long
voyage, the place of abode of the friend I crossed the
Atlantic to visit. How far I have wandered during
these five months, and how little I imagined, on
setting out, the distance to which my tour would
extend ! My last letter was closed at the moment
we were nearing St. Lucia, the beautiful, but deadly.
We anchored for a few hours in the harbour of
Castries, the principal town. It is difficult to believe
that danger or death can lurk in anything so lovely.
I never beheld a scene more magically beautiful
than this, the moon at the time shedding her soft
light over land and sea. Yet the history is too universal and too often repeated to be false, which tells
us that fever, miasma, and death are the habitual
guests in this plague-stricken isle, which nevertheless
looks like what we may suppose the garden of Eden
to have been. Alas for romance ! the only real

resemblance between Paradise and St. Lucia is the "trail of the serpent over all." Speaking seriously, the plague of serpents, scorpions, and every description of poisonous reptile, is so deadly, that even I, who am not easily turned aside from visiting or exploring strange or new places, have relinquished all idea of landing at St. Lucia, though it will be daylight on the occasion of our next visit. A little before sunset to-day, the coast of Barbados was clearly discernible, soon after we entered Carlisle Bay, in which lies Bridgetown, the place of our destination. What an extraordinary and almost incredible difference there is between the external appearance of this and the island I have been describing to you in the beginning of my letter! The approach to Barbados, it must be owned, is as nearly approximating to ugly as anything in nature can. Flat, white, sandy, chalky! This does not sound picturesque, and it *is* still less so. In short, I was very forcibly reminded of the Sussex shore near Brighton, but without the town of Brighton to make amends for the dreary rest of the scene. We anchored about eight o'clock, and were, to my great joy, almost immediately *boarded* by my friend's husband and several other old acquaintances in the 36th, whom I had not met since we spent the winter in the Ionian Islands.

January 5th.—We have now been a week at

Barbados, chiefly occupied in joining the festivities
incidental to the Christmas and New Year time.   I
had always heard a great deal of Barbadian hospitality, and I may very sincerely say that it has more
than equalled my anticipations.   As I cannot give
you a detailed account of when and where each fête
took place, I must just note down dinners, rides,
balls, picnics, &c., as they come to my recollection.
But first of all I will give you a sketch of our abode.
A charming little yellow cottage, bungalow-shaped,
and raised from the ground by a few steps, but once
inside, no going up or down stairs; all the rooms are
en suite.

Whilst sitting in the drawing-room, by the bye,
windows and doors being always open, we are constantly charmed by the visits of the most exquisite
little humming-birds, who dart through the room—
in at one window and out at another, like a flash of
lightning.   The cottage is enclosed in a small but
very pretty garden or rather shrubbery, where grow
many a flower and tree unknown to us except in
hothouses; one particularly, of which I have yet to
learn the name, serves the creole ladies as a ball-
dress decoration.   The leaves, instead of being green,
are a rich scarlet, and being of a very velvety texture
one can sew them on to a white dress, and thus make
an inexpensive, and, to a brunette, a becoming
toilette.   Mrs. P. has come in laden with a complete

garniture for Eleanor and herself, to be used at General Wood's ball to-night. We rode on horseback, a few mornings back, to a village called Speightstown, about three miles distant, and returned to be present at the parade of the regiment, a ceremony which, as in the Mediterranean, afforded an opportunity for the gathering together of all the *beau monde* and otherwise. Speightstown seemed to me to be only inhabited by negroes. I have seldom been more amused than by this ride, the exceeding drollery of appearance they all present, their talk, their impudence, the songs they improvise about yourself while passing them. The way they set about doing everything is so perfectly ludicrous, I could not help fancying them a lot of baboons got up as a travestie on men and women. Received yesterday a letter and cards from the Governor of Barbados, Sir W. Colebrooke, and his daughters, apologising for not calling in person, owing to illness of the former. With this exception, I think we have already made the acquaintance of the island. At a dinner party given a few days ago, I tasted the renowned Barbadian dish called "Pepper-pot," and think it well deserves all the laudation it receives. I was rather surprised at finding it was served hot,—I do not know why, but I had always fancied it was a cold galantine sort of edible. However, it is very good. It is made of fish, flesh, and fowl, I believe—a kind of gipsy *pot au feu*—things being added day by day. *"Casarip,"* a condiment resembling Harvey's sauce and anchovy, is a principal ingredient in flavouring the whole. While on the subject of eating and cooking, I must not forget to mention one of the greatest delicacies in the West Indian cuisine, namely, "land crabs." There is a regular season for them. They come in swarms at one part of the year, and cross over the land. They go over everything in their way, not turning aside for houses, but go up the walls and across the roof. Of course plenty are stopped on the road and prematurely cut off from further prosecuting their travels. They are, when stuffed and well seasoned, remarkably good eating.

4th.— We had a brilliant ball last night. The general commanding the forces out here, General Wood, with his wife and daughters, were the hosts. There was a good sprinkling of the navy, which made a pretty variation with the red coats, also several of the Barbadian families settled here; the rooms were beautifully decorated with cactus, ferns and other tropical plants, which, together with coloured lights peeping from the shrubberies outside, heightened the beauty of the scene exceedingly.

10th.—Just returned from a picnic excursion at "Scotland," a part of Barbados about fourteen miles from hence, which bears this rather grandiloquent denomination. I believe the name was conferred originally on this place from its being of a slightly mountainous or rather hilly character, besides being the only bit of "scenery" of which poor Barbados can boast. It is, however, remarkably picturesque, a bluff headland of steep rock jutting out into the sea. A path, or rather I should say steps, are hewn in this rock, in the crevices of which grow aloes, oleander, cactus, and lastly *heather!* So "Scotland" is not such a' misnomer after all. To descend these steps to the sea shore, and thence enjoy both the view and the fresh breeze, is the favourite *passe-temps* whilst the chickens and champagne are getting ready on the heathery sward above. The spot chosen for our repast was under the shade of some fine cabbage palms, with a view in the distance of Codrington College, a sort of priests' seminary for Church of England men, endowed by Colonel Codrington. Our picnic was scarcely ended before unfortunately there came one of those tropical storms of rain of which Europeans have little notion. We had all to fly wherever we best could at a moment's notice; and as it was, some of our party did not escape a severe wetting. Those who came off best had taken refuge among the sugar-canes of a neighbouring field, which from their height and thickness afforded tolerable protection.

I think by this time you will be of opinion that

L 4

my letter is long enough, so I will close and despatch
it at once, resuming my adventures, perhaps, in about
a week's time.

Ever your affectionate, .

C.

CHAPTER XXXIX.

Barbados, January 15th.—My dear Father,— Our very agreeable stay here is fast drawing to an end. The island steamer, which will convey us away, is expected in two days more, so we are making the best use of the short time that remains. We were present a few nights ago at a coloured ball given by the soldiers of the West India Regiment, quartered here. They had invited both their own officers and those of the 36th, with their wives and families. It was a curious spectacle—at least it appeared so to me, as I cannot yet familiarise myself to the sight of black *ladies* (as they are very tenacious of being called) in delicate-coloured ball-dresses. I was so amused on the morning of this ball night at being called in very mysteriously by one of Mrs. P.'s women-servants, who requested I would accompany her into her bed-room. I went—and beheld spread out on the sofa two wonderful dresses, one a canary-coloured tarlatane with four flounces and a profusion of bows of riband, and the other a deep rose-coloured silk,

ornamented with green leaves. Between these two
" Lydia" begged I would give my opinion which
would " *become* " her best, and she promised to abide
by my decision. It was a grave dilemma; however,
I decided in favour of the tarlatane, thinking black
and yellow would probably look better than black,
pink, and green. She seemed quite satisfied and
danced merrily in the evening, and I only hope she
felt convinced that she was the belle of the room.
Next day we took a drive to visit some friends residing at White Park, about five miles from Bridge
Town. Though there is, with the exception of Barbadian Scotland, very little striking scenery in the
island, yet the near view of the country is pretty
enough. There are flowers in profusion to be had
for the trouble of gathering, and I was tempted many
times on our way to White Park to jump out of the
pony chaise to load myself with the spoils of the
hedgerow. Jessamine and passion-flowers are the
most abundant. On our return we drove into Bridge
Town. There is little, however, deserving of note here.
The shops are poor-looking; still the contents are
better than those of the other islands, I believe. The
principal " place " is called Trafalgar Square, and
has a statue of Nelson. The Cathedral is a tolerably
good-looking building, and the Barracks of St. Anne
are large, well built, and provided with every comfort
required for the soldiers. They have only very lately

returned to these barracks, as last year, in consequence
of both yellow fever and cholera breaking out, the
soldiers were all removed into tents on the high
parade-ground, and lived there encamped for many
months, until all was restored to its original healthy
condition in the island.

16th.—We have just returned from the last visit
to be paid in Barbados, as our time of departure is
near at hand. This excursion was to dine and spend
the day with the family of a planter, Mr. C——, who
entertained us at their country house. I have enjoyed
myself exceedingly. The amusements were varied;
besides walking about the beautiful gardens, there was
dancing, swinging in hammocks, and floating on the
lake in small canoes. The dinner was given on purpose to show us all the peculiarities of the best West
Indian cookery. We had callipash and callipee,
pepper-pot and land crabs, turtle steaks and hot
pickles, yams and sweet potatoes, and salad made of
the aguacate pear. Then for fruit, guavas, guava
jelly, pomegranates, sapotes, custard apples, forbidden
fruit, and the above-mentioned aguacate pears. I
have taken some trouble to try and obtain some reliable information as to how aguacate should be spelt,
but I am by no means sure even now that I have
succeeded. By some it is called avocado, by others
aquacada, and lastly aguacate. I have chosen this,
as, in the few instances where any attempt at giving

a derivation has been made, it was observed there
was something about water; therefore, assuming the
derivation to be Spanish, " agua," being the translation of " water," is, I think, the more correct term of
the two. The English people, however, cut the Gordian
knot by calling it by the singular appellation of
" subaltern's butter." For this there *is* a reason, and
not a bad one. Butter is not very good and is very
dear in the West India islands, but this aguacate pear
makes a very good substitute, and at a very small
cost. The taste is very like ordinary fresh butter
in which a little oil has been mixed. Eaten with
plenty of bread it is very good, or made into a salad,
as we had it to-day, with a little salt, pepper, mus-
tard, and vinegar; but it is far too rich to eat alone as
a fruit.

17*th.*—Took leave of hospitable Barbados and our
numerous friends. A parting compliment was paid
to us by the 36th Regiment, whose officers themselves
manned a boat and rowed us to the steamer, which
was waiting in Carlisle Bay, while part of the band
followed in another boat playing " Should old acquaintance be forgot."

20*th.*—Though now we have not on this our return trip left the steamer, it has been a great pleasure
to see again the fairy islands, for without exaggeration they may well be called so. Their beauty does

not pall on the eye or the taste. Seen from the water
I am not sure that the little island of St. Kitt's should
not rank next to St. Lucia in picturesque and wild
scenery; but it would be a difficult task, putting Barbados of course *hors de combat,* for any one to decide
which particular one of the Antilles should be termed
the most beautiful. It being daylight on this occasion, I was sorely tempted, *malgré* the serpents, to
invade St. Lucia, it is so wondrously beautiful; and
the day more than fulfilled the promise of the night.
The two " Pitons," high sharp-pointed rocks, rising
from the centre of the land straight into the clouds
apparently, are most imposing objects. They are
said to be quite inaccessible to human feet, and, as
usual with any such natural phenomena, frightful
legends exist concerning them. The most generally
accredited story is that they are guarded by Py-
thons, *alias* boa constrictors, who deal summarily
with any one rash enough or unfortunate enough
to attempt penetrating into their fastnesses. Two
foolhardy English sailors are said to have furnished
the last examples. They departed, determined to
ascend " le Gros Piton," and never were heard of
more. However, all things considered, I used that
discretion said to be the better part of valour, and
can only indulge the hope that it is " distance lends
enchantment to the view." We entered the bay of

St. Thomas this evening, now become a familiar
scene. To-morrow we set out on our southern expedition; and as the "Parana" sails for England again
early in the morning, I shall send you this letter
by her.

Ever your affectionate,

C.

CHAPTER XL.

Navy Bay, January 27th. — My dear Father,—
After a voyage of nearly a week's duration, we
landed here about midday. Though but a small
place (in point of size, indeed, it is scarcely more
than a village), this enjoys the distinction of having
no less than three names: Navy Bay by the English,
Colon by the Spanish, Aspinwall by the Americans,
are the appellations severally bestowed on it. The
aspect of the town is singular. The houses look like
a collection of booths, or those cardboard houses
made for children's toys, into the very midst of
which, as I was contemplating the scene, came
shrieking and whirling the Panama train, with its
odd *reversed*-looking chimney, bringing back vividly
to my recollection the cars of the " blessed States."
We are about to bid adieu for a time to the Atlantic
and the " Bonnie Dee," here, and to try our fortunes
on the Pacific. As we have but a short time to spare,
I shall send you the diary I have written since
leaving St. Thomas; meanwhile I must try and get

some information concerning things in general, connected with our future movements. It seems very strange that notwithstanding the pretty constant communication which now takes place between the two sides of the Isthmus, so little intelligence can be obtained about the South Pacific route. All that I can positively make out is, that the steamboats bound for Lima and Valparaiso leave Panama on the 7th and 21st of each month; but for all details I must wait till we are across the Isthmus.

On the 21st of January we left St. Thomas at daylight, a very high wind, almost a gale, blowing. In a few hours we were out of sight of land.

24th.—We were aroused this morning before five o'clock, in order to see the sun rise upon the Sierra Nevada, and to enjoy the first sight of the continent of South America. I could just discern the snow edging the sharp summits of the mountain chain ; but unfortunately the sun, although generally rather too bright than too dim in these climes, was to-day enveloped in vapour and mist, and although he went through the ceremony of rising, he lacked the brilliancy which usually distinguishes him. This Sierra Nevada is a branch of the great chain of the Andes, and is called La Sierra de Santa Martha, at the town of which we arrived about 10 A.M., and anchored in the bay. I was both surprised and delighted at the magnificent spectacle which met my eyes on going on deck. Not having heard any one talk of or praise Santa Martha particularly, I was totally unprepared for such a scene. I think the voyage well worth the trouble between St. Thomas and this, even were we to see nothing else. Hills that without any exaggeration might well be called mountains rise straight up from the water's edge. The waves dash themselves in fury against the rocky shore, whilst all around, far as the eye can reach, peak rises above peak, of every imaginable form, till they are gradually lost in the clouds. Captain Parker allowed us time to go on shore, and we took a walk all about the town for upwards of an hour. But there is literally nothing to be seen in it; even the cathedral was closed, and the whole place seemed deserted. The heat of Santa Martha surpasses all I ever experienced or suffered elsewhere. After perambulating the town for as long as we were able to endure baking, we took boat again, and returned home to the " Dee," when we gladly accepted the refreshment of some iced champagne and seltzer-water after our fatiguing excursion. It is blowing tremendously, but I understand it is by no means unusual weather on this part of the coast. We proceeded on our voyage at sunset to-day, and hope to reach Cartagena in the morning. We have left at Santa Martha a large party who had made the voyage from St. Thomas with us,—an English merchant and his family, who are going to settle at Bogota. They expect to reach the latter in eight days. They will have several hundred miles' travelling on the great Magdalena river, but I should fear will meet many difficulties, as, besides a tolerably numerous party in themselves, children, and servants, they comprehend a small edition of Noah's ark, horses, dogs, cows, sheep, poultry; also carriages, carts, saddles, and bridles.

25th.—We did not, after all, arrive at Cartagena until nearly five o'clock P.M., for although the wind was fair it was anything but light, and the swell was tremendous. I was not sorry for the delay, however, as it enabled us to see by daylight what is generally passed in the middle of the night, namely, the mouth of the great river Magdalena. As I unfortunately missed " the father of waters " in the north, the Mississippi, being too " yellow-feverish," I am glad at least to have the opportunity of beholding one of the principal South American rivers. One would hardly guess the Magdalena at its embouchure, however, to be anything but a lake : indeed, it is difficult at first to distinguish it from the ocean which it joins. Our first view of Cartagena was just " in the light of declining day." From the sea its appearance is very fine, and greatly reminded me of

the appearance of Venice from the lagunes. In order
to enter the harbour of Cartagena a great detour
must be made, by which, to all appearance, the city
is left far behind. We steamed along a narrow
channel called the Boca Chica, or little mouth, and
after proceeding for about nine miles, but in perfectly smooth water, in an exactly contrary direction
to our previous course, we suddenly found ourselves
in the bay, where our good ship speedily anchored
herself. A very curious hill or mountain rises immediately above this town, and is called the "Popa,"
from its resemblance to the prow of a ship. We
have not been able to see much of the city of Cartagena, as, by the time the indispensable preliminaries
were settled attendant on the arrival of the packet,
the mails landed, and matters in order, it was
sunset. We went on shore, however, and were introduced by Captain Parker to the English Consul, Mr.
Kortright, with whom we spent the evening; he has
a delightful house, with a gallery going round it,
whence one looks down upon the most refreshing
green shrubs and brilliant-hued flowers: and apropos
of hues, he possesses a beautiful and, I should think,
most valuable collection of birds all netted here, that
is to say in New Granada, of which republic Cartagena is the seaport, and Bogota the capital. It is
scarcely possible to imagine or believe, without see-

ing, the wonderful variety of shades and tints, shining and sparkling like gems, on the wings of these lovely creatures. I must not omit to mention also a very magnificent preserved butterfly, which was under a glass shade, ornamenting Mr. Kortright's drawing-room table, measuring upwards of twelve inches from wing to wing, of a glowing cobalt-blue colour, spotted with silver. Our host has kindly volunteered to show us some of the lions of Cartagena to-morrow morning, provided the powers that rule the " Dee " and her movements should be propitious and allow us a few hours; or if not, the engagement is to hold good on our return next month.

26th.—We were obliged to relinquish our intended drive into the country this morning, as the " Dee " was up, steam and all, betimes, and we got under way between eight and nine A.M. Wind still high, and the swell great, but not quite so bad as it has been.— To resume my letter. We have now located our-selves for to-day at the " City Hotel," a wonderful structure made entirely of wood, not thicker than pasteboard. I do not at all fancy sleeping in such a place, for fear of its catching fire. Nevertheless we shall be under the necessity of doing so for one night. We have just been introduced to a Mr. Stevenson, the stepson of Mr. Cowan, the English Consul. He is going to-morrow, and has kindly undertaken to chaperone us in our journey across the Isthmus.   So now farewell.   I will, if all be well, send you a letter from Panama.   The heat here is intense, far greater than we have yet experienced anywhere in the course of our wanderings.

Ever your affectionate,

C.

CHAPTER XLI.

January 28*th, Navy Bay.*—My dear Father,—Although I shall not send this letter till we are on the other side of the Isthmus, I shall resume my notes at once, partly for occupation's sake, especially during this long day of waiting here. Shortly after the despatch of my last, the signal for sailing was made, and at length came the parting hour, when the friends and companions of many a weary mile were to leave us, and the farewell was spoken. I can hardly describe to you the feeling of desolation which we experienced for a short period as we watched the "Dee" till she gradually faded out of sight, then turned to find ourselves quite alone, standing between two oceans and two continents. Our solitary reflections were, however, soon unceremoniously interrupted by the clamorous tones of the dinner bell, and being driven in to feed in a style more than ever reminding me of the States. By the time we reached the dinner-room we found the hungry claimants had already nearly cleared the tables, and very shortly after they had vanished from the scene as well as the food, with a celerity which had something of the miraculous.

29th.—Embarked on the railroad, though in rather a novel mode of conveyance, namely, the baggage waggon. But it was Sunday, and the good Yankees were *too* good to accommodate passengers with a carriage on that day, though they sent a luggage car; but then if they had not done that, sundry *dollars* would have been sacrificed, and so they pocketed their principles to the extent of forwarding the " Dee's " cargo, and also allowed us by a great favour, and in consideration of our paying *first-class* prices, to sit on our boxes in the said waggon. We preferred doing this, however, and having the advantage of Mr. Stevenson's escort, to waiting till the next day, and coming with the crush of Californians who were expected to arrive by the American steamer. The road is a narrow cutting through heavy masses of damp rich-looking jungle, with interminable forests spreading far and wide in the distance, and all covered and interlaced with the same sort of beautiful creepers and parasites we had so much admired in Mexico. In about two hours we reached a small " station " or settlement, consisting of two or three small Indian huts called *Caravali.* Here we left the railroad, which however is open some distance further (as far as Gorgona); but our chaperon having his own boat, and always employing this

means of conveying the silver and "treasure," as it
is called, with which he is intrusted by the company,
we embarked with him on the river Chagres.
During the delay which took place here while the
cargo was being shipped, we had an amusing scene.
The wildness and novelty of the whole affair induced
me to attempt a little sketch. First came ourselves
seated on a plank under the shade of a tree, then the
winding river, the odd-shaped canoes, and the all
but naked boatmen, some sleeping, a few working,
some eating, and others taking sudden plunges into
the water and diving like ducks. Close to ourselves
the occupations were still more varied. The extra-
ordinary-looking Indian women were several of them
cooking soup and other savoury messes on a very
primitive sort of *batterie de cuisine,* consisting of a
few sticks laid on a few stones, and a black mysterious-
looking cauldron crowning the whole edifice, out of
which pot-luck was doled to all suppliants by the
various artistes,—I cannot call them "fair," as their
complexions varied from a bright chocolate colour to
the deepest jet. But their costume was truly unique—
full-dress low bodices and short sleeves to their gowns,
their woolly locks hanging in wild luxuriance about
their necks and shoulders, and profusely ornamented
with natural flowers, beads, combs, gold and silver.
By way of variety, another group, composed of some
half-dozen people, were occupied playing cards as if

for their lives, so intent were they on their game.
These looked especially picturesque, as, in order to
shield themselves from the burning rays of the sun,
they had thrown a boat's sail over three or four
poles, and under its shade they had encamped themselves. I had begun to try and sketch with my
pencil a few of the principal points in this tableau,
when one or two of the Indians having perceived
what I was about, gave utterance to some exclama-
tions of astonishment, which speedily attracted the
whole community round me, and then ensued a
really laughable scene, which, I take it, quite exemplifies the vanity inherent in our human nature.
They *all*, men as well as women and children, began
to put themselves into what they considered the most
engaging and favourable attitudes, and begged I
would take their likenesses. At last, the boat being
ready, we embarked in it, and had a somewhat
tedious voyage up the river for five hours to Cruces,
which is to be our halting place for the night. The
mode used in navigating the Chagres, is poling, a
most laborious as well as slow proceeding, but I suppose it must be the only feasible plan, as surely, were
another method practicable, it would have been tried
before now. Notwithstanding this disadvantage, it
must be owned that the scenery, and all surrounding
the banks of the river Chagres, is so wonderful and
so interesting in its own peculiar style, that were the

M

discomforts and drawbacks ten times worse than they
actually are, I think the voyage well worth the experiment. The sun I must own was almost over-
powering: it is a wonder we did not get a stroke,
being exposed to five hours' unceasing blaze. I never
before to-day completely realised "the deep silence
of a noontide forest." * Far as the eye could reach
over hill and over plain, before and around, spread
the undulating but unbroken surface of the tropical
woods, looking like some vast petrified ocean (I was
going to say frozen, but the idea of ice in such a
scene would be too "far fetched"). Then the stillness, not a breath, not a sound was heard, save what
was caused by ourselves, and that was but little, for
it was too hot to talk or to move unnecessarily,
therefore the only actual token of life was the measured plashing of the pole in the water drawing us
slowly along. We had proceeded thus for a couple
of hours when we experienced an interruption of a
very curious nature, and which, owing to the incon-
gruity it presented to all that had gone before, will
not be speedily forgotten. Our boat suddenly stopped at the entrance to a little creek, when there appeared by the river side — a woman! with a child of
between four and five years old. One would have
imagined she had dropped from the skies, did the

* Disraeli, "Sybil."

inhabitants of the celestial regions dress in the style of this lady; but where on the surface of the earth she did come from, was certainly neither to be seen nor conceived. She wore a pale yellow dress of crape gauze, or some equally light material, with several blonde flounces of most elaborately designed patterns, Over her shoulders was thrown a shawl, bright blue in colour, and also of some light material, while neck, arms, and head shone resplendent with jewels (chiefly diamonds) and flowers. To complete the picture, she held in her hands some articles of furniture generally supposed to belong rather to the bedroom than the public conveyance. I wish the climate had been cooler. I should have so much liked to enter into conversation with her; but it was too hot, and as she did not utter a word, I feared that even if I tried Spanish, I should not be successful as the patois are many and various. We found ourselves equally lethargic when, a little later, the boatmen darted quickly across the river in pursuit of an unhappy iguano, which they espied basking in the sun. Having caught the poor victim, they tied him up, fastening the claws behind the back, and so carried him in triumph, preparatory to cooking and eating him. In point of size, the iguano seems to be midway between a large lizard and a small alligator. The flesh is considered in these parts a table delicacy. At length we reached our haven,

Cruces, a villanous looking little place. On disembarking, we walked through the village, a collection of tumble down log huts, till we arrived at our sleeping quarters, the huts so called. Here I cannot say we slept, but we passed the night. Besides the agreeable sight of monstrous spiders, innumerable in quantity, attached to the walls and ceiling of our rooms, scorpions were more than *suspected;* and to crown all, we were gratified by hearing a mysterious hissing during the whole night, which the next morning we were informed was produced by *snakes.* A pleasant and enjoyable residence certainly! Among other discomforts we were starved; there was absolutely nothing to eat; no bread, no fresh meat, only some dried beef, which was totally unmanageable, and there was not even chocolate; but by way of compensation, there was any quantity of claret and brandy: so, although we were faint from want of food, we were obliged to bear the deprivation as best we could, and at ten o'clock on the morning of the 30th we mounted our mules to accomplish the rest of the Isthmus passage, a distance of about twenty-one miles. From the different accounts I had heard and read of the perils and dangers of the road, I had gone fully prepared for no end of catastrophes and adventures of all kinds, and consequently I was really half disappointed to find so little need for all my powers of endurance. To begin with the road:

there was scarcely a single spot on our path to-day that
I would not have ridden even a good English horse
over; and with our little Mexican steeds we should
easily have gone over the ground in less than half
the time it took us toiling and jogging on these
indolent mules.   There must, however, be some
wonderful difference caused by even a day's rain.
We, with our usual good fortune in the way of
weather, have had nothing but "plenty too much "*
sunshine all the way.   And it seems impossible that
every one should concur in describing the difficulties
of the passage as so great, were there not some
grounds for apprehension.   I remember, too, Lord
S. (whose correct and graphic account of the rest of
the trip has been most invaluable to me) mentions
that, at nearly every step, his mule got up to its neck
in a bog or quagmire of some sort.   Certainly a very
different state of things to what we experienced,
everything being dry, parched, and burning.   After
about eight hours' slow progress, we at length gained
the summit of a hill, from whence the broad Pacific,
the islands, and the beautiful bay and town of Panama
burst upon our sight.   It would be hard to find a
more lovely view as it "shone in the light of declining day."

   31st, *Panama.*—Our ideas of rest and peace, if

---

* A favourite Nigger expression.

we had any, were but rudely dispelled on arriving
here. We had been a little prepared during our
passage of the Isthmus, by encountering from time
to time some parties of frightfully uncouth and
savage-looking people (who all asked us an infinite
number of questions), for a certain amount of annoyance and discomfort on a nearer acquaintance with
the Californians. But, alas! the reality far surpassed
our imaginations. We had the ill luck to fall into
the cross tide of gold diggers to the number of upwards of 1600 *savages* just landed simultaneously on
either side of the Isthmus. No tongue and no pen
could do them justice; their appearance was scarcely
human, and as to their manners, I must renounce all
attempts to give an account of them. One *small*
item I shall note down as being the *first* specimen.
On leaving my bed-room at the hotel, and coming
into the public (called *par excellence* the *ladies*)
saloon. I found tables, sofas, and floor covered with
bones, fat, and sundry other remains of food, which
the savages, whose shouts and whooping had been dis-
turbing me for two hours previously, had been de-
vouring without other implements than those already provided by nature, namely tooth and nail.
Fortunately I had a letter of introduction to Mr. and
Madame Hurtado (the latter is the daughter of Mr.
Perry, our consul here), and, thanks to their kindness
and hospitality, we are enabled to avoid the annoy-

ances of this hotel during the day, as we are invited to take our meals and spend the day with them, as long as we remain at Panama. But the nights are unendurable; no sleep, no peace. Moreover, the charges are positively ridiculous. For one wretched little room containing a bed and a half, the *half* being a bed without a mosquito net, which constitutes by far the most important moiety in these parts, one cracked water jug and basin, and one looking glass, they demand the preposterous sum of five dollars a night; food, lights, &c., extra.

February 1*st.* — This morning we visited the cathedral, almost the only building worthy of notice in the town which is not gone to decay. It is a fine old edifice, with some good specimens of sculpture. There are many other ruined churches, convents, and houses, all bearing traces of much past grandeur and magnificence. But the great charm of Panama is the scenery. All around, the bay, the sea, the sky, the distant mountains, all is enchanting, far more like the Greek islands than any other part of the world I have seen since leaving them.

3*rd.*—We find that the steamer for the south does not leave here until the 7th of this month, consequently we have decided on going to the island of Taboga for the time yet to elapse, so we shall go there to-morrow. One very great pleasure I have enjoyed since coming here, which has gone far to

make up for the disagreeables of the hotel.   Every
night in walking back from Mr. Hurtado's, I have
paused to gaze on the Southern Cross shining in all
its splendour above us.

4*th, Taboga.*—On board the R. M. S. ship
Bogota.   We have been very kindly received by
Captain Hall the commander of this beautiful
vessel, and allowed to take up our quarters on board
at once, instead of stopping on shore.   I am greatly
pleased with this island, the air is fresher and cooler
than at Panama, and yet we have the beautiful view
of the bay and surrounding country.   We went this
afternoon on a shilling expedition on the golden
sands of Taboga; we picked up some beautiful and
rare specimens.   The Pacific coast is very famous for
its conchological (if there be such a word) productions.   Not very far distant are the Pearl Islands,
whence a considerable trade is obtained from the
pearl fishery.   At Panama, I saw several very
curiously wrought ornaments, in seed pearl and
gold filagree, which had the advantage at least of
being very uncommon; also the famous Panama
chains of pure unalloyed gold, flexible as a blade of
grass.

6*th.*—The Bogota returned to Panama to receive
the mails and passengers; we have therefore come on
shore to spend the day with the Hurtados.   We set
out on our travels once more to morrow.   As I do not

know when the next opportunity of sending you any
tidings will be, I shall post this now here, and until
we arrive at Lima will write a journal of all that
occurs.   In the mean time I am ever your affectionate

C.

CHAPTER XLII.

Panama, February 7th, 6 P.M. — We have just quitted the harbour, my dear Father, on our southern voyage; weather fine, but excessively hot. A very disagreeable incident occurred yesterday evening on board this vessel, which has caused me great vexation ; a morocco travelling case of mine, which I valued highly, not on account of its own worth, but because it had belonged to my mother, was stolen from my cabin. I immediately communicated the intelligence to the captain, and since then everything has been done which was possible to discover the thief or get the case restored, but as yet without effect. I have offered a reward of 100 dollars, and no questions asked, if it is returned to me ; and Captain Hall, by my persuasion, has promised pardon to the culprit if he will now confess ; or, as there might be a feeling of shame connected with his comrades were he to own he was a robber, a particular spot in the ship will be visited twice a day, and if the case is put there no inquiries will be made. In the meantime the officers of the ship are told off in different directions to search the berths and quarters of the crew.

8*th.*—They have got hold of a man who acknowledges he knows something of my lost property, but who is foolish enough to be obstinate, and refuse any further explanation. As he bears a very bad character, and is strongly suspected to be himself the thief, Captain Hall has given him till midday to confess what he knows or has done, and if he does not before that, he will be put in irons. To my consternation the foolish man has proved stubborn, and consequently the threatened punishment has been inflicted. We crossed the line at 7 P.M. this evening. Heat very great, though perhaps not quite so violent as I expected. The days are gone by now when crossing the line was an event celebrated by a mimic visit from Neptune. Now the fact was merely stated, and we found ourselves *sans cérémonie* in the southern hemisphere.

10*th.*— I am happy to say that the prisoner has made a confession, and, above all, that my case is restored safe and sound. The reason, or more properly speaking the temptation, which he alleged prompted the theft he has now disclosed. I had been a good deal puzzled about this part of the business, as I had not lost anything which would fetch any money to speak of; but it seems that, during the few days

M 6

we had spent on board the ship at Taboga, my proceedings had been watched, and by this means the
man had discovered that I was in the habit of keeping my purse and a small box containing rings (one
of which was a diamond) inside the stolen case, and
these were the objects of his desire. Very fortunately
for me, however, he had *not* observed that every
evening, on going to dress for dinner at six o'clock,
I put the rings on my fingers and the purse in my
pocket, the latter because we generally played at
vingt-un every night between tea and bedtime; and
from not having noticed this he abstracted the case
at eight o'clock. Had he taken it during the day,
both ornaments and money would then have gone, I
fear, irretrievably. As it was, the only loss I have
sustained is that of three or four very long letters
addressed to people at home, and which were all
ready sealed and prepared for departure, and these
the thief very wantonly threw into the sea instead of
the post. Very fortunately, your letter escaped, from
my having written it while on shore. But "all's well
that ends well," and I am pleased enough to have
escaped so well. The next thing will be to prevail
on Captain Hall to pardon and set free the delin-
quent, whose stupidity I think far exceeds his crimi-
nality. The idea of letting himself be found out,
when, according to the bargain, he might have
restored the case to me with or without making any

explanation, and, unquestioned, would have received 100 dollars! Now that my mind is easy on this subject I can take time to chronicle an incident which took place on the morning of our departure from Panama, and which might have rendered it a matter of indifference whether the morocco case was found or not. Much against my inclination and judgment, I was persuaded to join a party in a sailing trip along the coast and bay, and for this purpose we embarked in a small cutter under the command of a gentleman whose name I will not mention, but who confessed he had never been in anything but a steamboat on the Pacific, and in this particular Bay of Panama knew nothing of the currents, swells, or any other peculiarities which might belong to it. This was not the most agreeable intelligence we could have received when about a hundred yards from the steamer. With the rashness and foolhardiness of ignorance, however, he proceeded to crowd every morsel of sail he could get hold of on the unlucky little boat, and, worse still, had *fastened* the principal sail as if he had intended to show off an experiment at the Polytechnic with manufactured perils. This feat was scarcely accomplished when over we went. What had exactly happened I know not, though I can form a tolerably good guess. On emerging from a most unwelcome dip in the sea, I saw a man with a knife in his hand (he was a sailor, not an officer), having cut loose the sail, my companion and myself looking like drowned rats, the "commander" and another gentleman looking very foolish, and a shark looking very much disappointed. So after this the rest of the party agreed with me it would be better to make no more such experiments, and to be contented with rowing quietly back. We had not proceeded long before we met one of the ship's boats, which the chief officer, Mr. Davies, sent off to our assistance, having seen through his telescope that something was wrong, though we were too far to enable him to distinguish the precise nature of the accident. Now to return to the present. Before midnight we entered the Guayaquil River, passing on our route a most singular island, called Dead Man's Island, from the extraordinary resemblance it bears to a dead person when laid out previous to burial.

11th, *Guayaquil.*—I had never till now *realised*, as the Americans would say, what heat was. Something quite indescribable, and with it all the rain is pouring in sheets. All about this territory, that is, in the neighbourhood of the Ecuador State, it very rarely ceases raining, while only about a hundred miles further down the coast it never rains at all. We went on shore and dined with the English consul and his family (Mr. Cox), having previously walked about the town and looked at the shops, which are not particularly famous. The celebrated hats called *par excellence* Panama, are all manufactured here. Guayaquil is also very celebrated for grass hammocks, woven with all sorts of pretty colours. I procured one of these as a souvenir. I must not forget to notice a production in which I imagine no other place in the world could vie with Guayaquil, namely, mosquitoes. I shall never forget the martyrdom I suffered during dinner; my neck, shoulders, arms, and feet are covered with stings as if I had the measles. Owing to the unfortunate thickness of the atmosphere we could not distinguish Chimborazo. We saw the dim outline of the Andes, however, and shall hope to have better fortune another day with Chimborazo, as in tolerably clear weather it is always visible from Guayaquil. *En revanche* for not seeing him, we enjoyed some ice at dinner brought that morning from his snowy peak.

12th.—Took our departure from Guayaquil very early this morning, rain pouring in torrents: passed again Dead Man's Island, and were still more struck with its strange form.

13th.—Touched at Payta, where, as the steamer was before her time, we remained some hours. We went on shore, and paid a visit to the consul, Mr. Blacker. This is a most deserted looking spot—nothing but sand hills, and a few houses, sand coloured, to be seen; nevertheless, it is I believe in a more flourishing condition than it looks. From the appearance of the sky, the inhabitants were rather anticipating a shower of rain — a luxury *they* had not enjoyed for *nine years!* We did not stay long enough to know whether their wishes were gratified or not.

14*th.* — At sea all day. Very early in the morning we passed the Lobos islands, of parliamentary and guano celebrity. I used often, when skimming over the papers at home, and the yarns they were spinning about Lobos, to wonder where on earth it was — little expecting I should so soon be on the spot.

15*th.* — Called at a small place called Pacasmayo — a very beautiful bay hemmed in by hills on every side, and the giant mountains in the distance. Some of our fellow passengers went on shore, and brought back with them some most magnificent grapes; bunches which would have gained a first class prize at the horticultural exhibitions.

16*th.*— Touched at Guacho, another of the numerous ports on the Pacific, and finally, about one o'clock P.M., anchored in the Bay of Callao, a busy looking place — flags of all nations, and vessels of all kinds; but the sky was dim and hazy. It is strange that, although it never rains in this land of the children of the sun, the sky is by no means generally clear; and I am told that the bright and cloudless blue, so often found in other parts of the two Americas, is here a great rarity. We landed at half past five P.M. at the railway station, which, like that at Navy Bay, is built at the water's edge. To make up for the thickness of the atmosphere when we arrived, there was a beautiful sunset, all crimson and gold, making even the sand hills and white rocks about Callao look romantic. Twenty minutes' drive brought us to the goal of our long journey, to Lima — the City of Kings. As we were accompanied by some of our shipboard friends, we proceeded on foot from the railway station to the hotel. The station, I should mention, was formerly an old convent, now transmogrified into a more worldly establishment. The first impression made by Lima, in the little we have been able to see this evening, is, that it bears a strong resemblance to Mexico. After walking the length of a handsome street, we suddenly emerged on the Plaza, and here I could quite have fancied myself back in the Aztec city. The cathedral occupies one entire side of the square, as it does in Mexico — but the other three sides are much gayer here. They are called portales, are ranged in arches, and something like the Palais Royal in point of gay shops and stalls, with all their wares spread out in tempting array, and brilliantly lighted. We have housed ourselves at Morin's hotel on the Plaza. The other hotel which was most recommended is quite full. There is a general rush from Callao and elsewhere in these parts to hear Catherine Hayes, who is to sing for the last time here to-night. She is *en route* to California. We were fortunately able to procure a box, and were soon gratified by hearing the Barbiere, Miss Hayes of course taking the part of Rosina. The opera house is pretty enough; still nothing very remarkable. But what *was* singular, was the almost exclusive British audience, so far away from home! There are many merchants settled here or in Callao, with their families; all of whom I imagine, attended on this occasion. Then there are two or three ships belonging to our navy, as well as the packet service. And each and all of these furnished a quota of dilettanti, eager to greet their countrywoman.

Having now safely landed, and established ourselves for a time at Lima, I shall close this letter, and hope to find an opportunity of sending it shortly. I should not wonder if you received it *viâ* California, as the communication is much more frequent that way by St. Jean de Nicaragua, than direct from here to England by Panama.

Ever your affectionate,

C.

CHAPTER XLIII.

Lima, Feb. 17th. — My dear Father,— The first day
of arrival at a resting place, however short that rest
is to be, I have hitherto observed, is always passed
in doing nothing. To-day has formed no exception
to our general course. After dinner we took a stroll
about the town, looked at the shops, and *voila tout.*
These are much finer than at Mexico; indeed, they
are so pretty as to almost deserve the modern title
given to Lima, namely, the Paris of South America,
though I still prefer the old one, Ciudad de los
Reyes, "The City of Kings." I have discovered
another great resemblance in Lima to Valetta, as
well as Mexico. The Peruvian and Maltese systems
of building covered balconies, chiefly of glass, outside every house, cause a striking similarity in the
appearance of the two cities. The churches here
are beautiful; we entered one, and were told it was
"La Merced." Some very rich carving round several
of the altars, and the exterior architecture very fine.

18*th.* — Walked to one of the public promenades

this evening, called the Alameda del Aepo. These Alamedas, wherever one meets them, all bear a strong family likeness one to another, whether at Havana, Mexico, Lima, or elsewhere: the same broad avenue for carriages, flanked by two narrower ones for equestrians and foot passengers; the only difference being in the description of trees with which they are planted. In this last respect Havana must literally bear the palm, as there one at least of the paseos is formed by palm trees, those fairest of the fair in woodland scenery. On our way we crossed the bridge over the Rimac, the river, or stream which waters the city, and from which its present name of Lima is said to have been derived, or rather corrupted. From this bridge; the view is, or should be, a very beautiful one; but it is seldom clear, a sad drawback.

19th. — Mr. Went, to whom I had brought a letter of introduction, sent his carriage, and we took a drive to the Valley of Amancaes, about three miles off. The same dull heavy sky above us, though the air was mild and soft. It really is difficult to believe that it never rains here. All this afternoon, had I been anywhere else, I should have pronounced a drenching shower as quite inevitable. Yet not a drop came, and none ever falls: that point all agree in *nem. con.* But some go as far as to say the sun never shines: this must be a little exaggerated; indeed, during the day, we have had a good deal: but sunshine without a cloud would be, I suppose, the miracle. I only wonder how the ancient people of the country came to be sun-worshippers, in a land where they saw him so little. From Amancaes the view of Lima is most imposing. Its numberless domes and towers, rising from the Pacific, lying peacefully beyond, reminds me of Byron's lines, speaking of Venice : —

> " She looks a sea Cybele fresh from ocean,
> Rising with her tiara of proud towers ;"

the strip of land intervening between Lima and Callao not being visible at this distance, and consequently Lima looks as if, like Venice, she rose from the waters. The valley of Amancaes itself is a most singular-looking spot, seemingly the bed of an extinct volcano, a wild sterile sort of plateau, surrounded by rocks and hills of lava of every sort of grotesque shape, not a shrub nor a blade of grass to be seen. Then the deathlike stillness of the air was something awful; not a sound to be heard. I could almost have fancied myself out of the world, and looking upon it. They say, however, that once a year, in the month of June, Amancaes bears a different aspect. On or about the festa of St. John, namely the 24th of June, there suddenly spring up in this desolate spot thousands, millions of golden coloured lilies! This savours rather of the mar-

vellous, but still they say it is true, and that so
suddenly does this change occur, that what is left
over night a parched and blackened desert, is found
in the morning clothed in gold. We fancied as the
sun began to set on our return (by the bye, he just
blazed out for about five minutes, in time to allow
him to make a decent exit), we thought we could
just descry the peaks of the Cordillera. I do hope
we shall have one good view of them before leaving.

20th.—Visited some of the churches, accompanied
by Mr. Pearson, the English clergyman. San
Domingo and the cathedral are both handsome-
looking buildings, but unfortunately there is not
much reality in either of them. This, however, is
inevitable, as they dare not build above a certain
height with any material more solid than reeds and
stucco, the earthquakes are so frequent. One which
occurred here about three weeks ago has nearly
shaken off the cross erected on one of the domes
of the cathedral, and it now stands all awry. In
one of the side chapels of this last-named edifice
there is a shrine of carved cedar wood, the most
beautiful specimen of workmanship I think I ever
saw; so fine and delicate that at first I imagined
it was ivory: indeed, even on a nearer inspection,
it more resembles ivory, the wood being of a sort
of pale cream colour; and this was carved into
wreaths, garlands, and festoons of flowers, inter-

twined one with another in the most marvellous manner. The high altar and some few other parts of the church are still decorated with silver columns and balustrades; but, like everything else in this part of the world, sadly shorn of its former splendour, and fast hastening to decay. Pizarro is said to be buried under the altar here. Strange that doubt should exist on such a subject, and I must own, even against my favourite Spaniards, that it speaks badly for their national gratitude, that the last resting-places of the two men to whom they owed the discovery of North and South America, Christopher Columbus and Francesco Pizarro, should be almost unknown; yet where their tombs are most generally supposed to be, the one in Havana and the other here, the small memorials that exist should be such wretched ones. Here there is more excuse, as they have renounced their allegiance to Spain, and consequently they view Pizarro's memory with no friendly feelings; but at Havana the case is different, and to Columbus they should erect a more noble monument.

21st.—Did not go out; received a few visits. Lima is suffering much at this time from an epidemic they call *peste*, and nearly every house has some sick people in it, rendering everything very *triste*, and the few who are well have all gone to Chorillas, a little bathing place a couple of leagues from the

town.   This *peste* appears to be a mild sort
of yellow fever, and has never appeared before in
Lima, which is generally reputed to be a most
healthy part of the world, and certainly has a most
delightful climate, at least to my taste.   The air is
warm without burning, and very soft.

22*nd.*—I have for the last two days been making
what I fear will turn out fruitless efforts to accomplish an expedition to Pachocamac, to see the ruins
of one of the great temples of the sun.   The distance
is but twenty-one miles, yet such is the indolence
of the people, that if it were one hundred, they
could not make more difficulties; to begin with,
they maintain that not less than three days are
necessary for the excursion, which really seems quite
ridiculous for so short a distance. 'However, it is
no use contending any more, and so we must put
up with riding out to-morrow and seeing some lesser
ruins which are more come-at-able.   We are fortunate
enough to be given a passage down to Panama in
the Virago, through the good-nature of Captain
Marshall her commander.   The advantages are many
in this arrangement.   First, the Virago does not
leave till Saturday, a day later than the mail steamer,
thus giving us a little more time to spend here;
then we shall avoid the numerous little ports along
the coast, which we have already sufficiently visited;
and lastly, we hope to go into the Bay of San Miguel,

the starting point of the Darien passage, and projected canal, and this vessel contains the members of the far-famed Darien expedition.

23rd.—Visited the church of San Pedro this morning, which, though the last, is the handsomest we have yet seen; the wood carvings in the side chapels are exquisite, and there are also some very tolerable pictures. We had previously gone to the museum, but it is a very poor affair, the only objects of any interest being a collection of the portraits of the Incas, from the two first children of the sun, Manco Capac and his wife, down to poor Atahualpa. It is of course to be conjectured that the artists have drawn chiefly on their imaginations, as it must be very doubtful that the Incas ever sat for their pictures. There are also a series of paintings representing the Spanish viceroys, beginning with Pizarro. Besides the portraits, I should mention three or four frightful looking mummies which are said to be the actual remains of some of the Incas of Peru, but the museum can boast of nothing more. I am rejoiced to say that we had this afternoon a superb view of the Andes in all their majesty and brightness. We stood on the Rimac bridge, and clearly traced the long outline of snowy peaks; so that hitherto unsatisfied desire is now accomplished, and off my mind. Passed the evening at the house of a lady to whom I was introduced by a mutual

N

friend, and who is universally talked of as "Mrs.
Smith of Lima." I suppose it must be from her
generous and universal hospitality; but to visit the
" City of Kings " and not know Mrs. Smith, "would
argue yourself unknown," besides being a serious personal privation. She has a charming house filled with
curiosities and rarities of all descriptions; but above
all she possesses the most astonishing and varied
collection of extraordinary plants and flowers. She
very good-naturedly gave me some rare specimens
of both flowers and leaves to preserve. The most
singular flower in her possession is one named "El
Espiritù Santo " (the Holy Spirit), of the Orchid
species. It is pure white, and in form nearly the
exact counterpart of a dove. I am told the plant
is exceedingly rare, not above two or three specimens
being in existence. At Mrs. Smith's house also was
the celebrated Madame Ida Pfeiffer, the female traveller, a quiet mannered and still more quiet featured
little person. Physiognomy is decidedly at fault
sometimes. No one would guess, to look at this
lady's impassive and rather expressionless countenance,
that she either had braved or was likely to brave
the dangers many and great of which she gives so
graphic an account in her " Voyage round the
World." She is now about to undertake a journey
in search of the source of the Amazon. The various
governments whose territories she explores, it must

be stated to their credit, give her every assistance
that lies in their power, though that is often un-
availing with some of their savage subjects. Madame
Pfeiffer has a son living at Munich, a doctor by
profession, and a great amateur of botany and
mineralogy. Mrs. S—— tells me that, repeatedly,
on being offered various substantial recompenses
for the benefits she has conferred by her useful
discoveries and · explorations, Madame Pfeiffer has
refused any other guerdon than a plant or some old
stones for the purpose of enriching the museum of
her beloved son. We tasted this evening a liqueur
called "Italia," made in Peru from a grape originally
brought from Italy; hence the name. Notwithstanding which, the taste is most decidedly whiskey-ish.
Barley must, I am sure, be partly used with the
grape in its manufacture.

23rd.—Employed this morning in shopping. The
ancient palace of Pizarro is now, alas! converted
into a Parisian looking "Passage," called by the
modern Peruvians "Portales." Here vendors of
of ponchos, gold and silver filigree work, sweet-
meats, and other luxuries do congregate. The
ponchos are generally handsome; they are made
of the Vicuña wool, soft to the touch- and brilliant
in hue, but not equal in my opinion to the Mexican
"serape." At 4 P.M. we mounted our horses. Took
a circuitous kind of ride for the purpose of exploring

several ruins; these mostly appear to have been temples to their divinity, or fortresses, each group of buildings being more or less surrounded by walls of the Cyclopean order. The great charm attaching to ruins in the old world, the Greek or the Roman for instance, is wanting here, I mean the broken column or "noble arch in proud decay." The constant dread of earthquakes causes everything intended to last to be built low and with a view to durability and solidity rather than beauty. One of our party to-day who has seen both, gives us the consolatory assurance that the ruins of the temple of the sun at Pachacamac are neither more extensive nor in better preservation than these.

24*th*. — Mounted again early this morning, on an excursion to Chorillos, about nine miles distant. This is the fashionable bathing place of Lima; and whither at the present moment all the inhabitants of the city have flocked, in order to be out of the way of the *peste*, and to enjoy the air, which is said to be purer and also cooler than at Lima. This last advantage *may* be the case, but it does not look so; indeed I never saw so apparently hot a looking place. A collection of huts all white, the rocks white, the ground under foot white, and the sea a burning blue. However, we spent the morning here, and saw the process of bathing. The people of both sexes go into the water together equipped in a kind of bloomer costume. The dressing rooms are singularly constructed. A number of them stand on the beach, and really resemble a miniature town. They are built of reeds, and are grouped in clusters, forming a complete labyrinth. Each little cell is provided with the requisite linen, and articles necessary to the toilette. In returning, we varied our route, passing through Miraflores, another, but inland watering place; this, however, is green and fresh looking, and I should think a much pleasanter and cooler summer residence than Chorillos. Since we have been at Lima, we have had daily at our dinner table the most delicious potatoes. The potato, if I remember rightly, is by origin a native of Peru. I have never anywhere met with any approaching these in flavour. It shows that cultivation does not always improve, though as in this case, it may enlarge. The Peruvian potatoes are small, not much exceeding a walnut in size, and of a bright yellow colour — very meally, and, as I have said, most excellent. They are served up as the centre dish of the table, ranged in a pyramid shape.

25th. — Bade farewell to Lima at seven o'clock this morning, taking the early train to Callao, where we found a boat from the Virago awaiting us, in which we immediately embarked, and in a few minutes were alongside of the pretty little steamer. Captain Marshall had invited the commander of the

Trincomalee, Captain Houston, to join us at breakfast before we sailed.   Callao * was looking far gayer,
and in all respects more attractive, than on the day
of our arrival.   This is somebody's birthday, too, so
the ships are dressed in all their gay colours.   About
ten o'clock the signal was given, and we were " off,
off and away."   Finding myself again on board a man
of war, recalls to my mind the cruises in the Bay of
Naples which I took some years back, when the
English and French fleets had gone there to bully
poor King Bomba.   The Virago is a pretty neat
little vessel, carrying six guns. ' She bears as her
motto on a conspicuous part of her (but not being
clever at nautical terms, I won't attempt to say
which), the words "England, Home, and Beauty."
There was some imitation of the ceremonies and
pranks which used of yore to inaugurate crossing the
line, on the day when this imaginary boundary
was passed.   It was made a sort of holiday on board
the ship, and several of the sailors enacted a sort of
masque or play, dressing themselves up as Neptune
and his satellites, marine monsters, and a few terrestrial donkeys closed the procession, which paraded
the decks for a considerable time, and saluted the
captain and officers.

   March 5th.—Anchored   once   more   at   Panama,

---

* I have abstained from alluding here to the hero of Callao, the
late Lord Dundonald; for who in England can need to be reminded
of one who, perhaps, unsurpassed even by Nelson, was equalled only
by the victor of the Shannon, the late Sir Philip Broke?

after a week's steaming from Callao — a pleasant voyage, delightful companions, in short, every thing *couleur de rose.* On our way, we lay for a few hours off Guayaquil, near the Dead Man's Island. I have now heard another version of the derivation of this name, which is in Spanish, " El Enamuerta-jado ;" namely, that some years ago there was an intention of building a lighthouse on the island to guide vessels in their course when near the mouth of the river. Four men were accordingly sent, with requisite building materials, and food to support them for six months, by which time the task was to be finished. In the meanwhile there occurred a "Pro-nunciamento," or revolution, or at any rate a change of government in the Ecuador State. Frequent as these events are, one might suppose that the general business of life would be carried on in the usual manner ; but if this tale be true, it would seem that the disturbance in question had obliterated the recol-lection of what had passed before. Time fled : the six months elapsed, and no one thought of the poor builders. At length a strange vessel on her way up or down the Pacific, descried a signal flying on the barren isle. She bore down upon it, and arrived in time to hear the tale of misery from one survivor out of the four. The rest had died starved to death, and this, the fourth, barely lived to complete his history, but sunk under the accumulated hunger and

N 4

exhaustion he had undergone.   I cannot help hoping,
however, that all this is a mere legend of romance;
and I am the more inclined to take this view of the
story, that the shape and outline of the land is so
unmistakably like a corpse enveloped in a shroud,
that it would seem amply sufficient to account for the
lugubrious name.   I had an opportunity of observing
on this occasion, what, owing to our having landed
so immediately on our previous visit to Guayaquil,
had then escaped me, viz. the curious water conveyance employed by the natives on this part of
the Pacific coast, called " balsas."   It is a strong
sort of raft, lashed securely together, and carries a
sail when required.   *Au reste* these balsas answer
the purpose of house, carriage, " kitchen, parlour, and
all."   We were a good deal amused, while awaiting the
time of our departure, in watching their manœuvres.
Several came round us, the occupiers trying to dispose
of their various wares, which included ponchos, straw
hats, monkeys, parrots, grass hammocks, fruit, and
flowers.   I have been watching the concoction of a
shocking dose which the doctor is preparing for our
benefit in crossing the isthmus, which is at present
much infected with "the fever" so called, and which, if
it once gets hold of you, they say it is rarely, if ever,
to be shaken off.   Dr. T.'s nostrum is a bottle of sherry,
in which he has infused such a quantity of quinine,
that it will demand a great deal of courage, both
moral and physical, to take his prescribed quantity,

which is a wine glassful every five miles. This is the native country of quinine, consequently it is procured here in all its strength and freshness. We have just heard that, to crown our good fortune, we beat the great mail steamer Sant Jago by three hours, though she had twelve hours start of us.

6th.— Landed this morning, and to our great regret, were obliged to say good-bye to Captain Marshall almost immediately, as he found it necessary to proceed to Darien (San Miguel) in the afternoon, to render assistance if need be, to the exploring party, from whom the last intelligence is very unsatisfactory. The Indians are evidently determined to resist to the death any attempt to penetrate into their territories. They have already resorted to the old savage expedient of shooting poisoned arrows from ambuscade. Having taken leave of Captain M. and the Virago's officers, we proceeded to Mr. Hurtado's, where we found a little daughter had been born since our last visit. We were also equally surprised to find Captain Parker awaiting us, he having crossed the isthmus in order to escort us back. I will now conclude this letter, having ended our pleasant Peruvian journey, and safely passed all perils in the Pacific. We must hope for equally good luck, during the remainder of our travel on the Atlantic. Your ever affectionate,

C.

CHAPTER XLIV.

Off Navy Bay, on board the Dee, March 7th. — My
dear Father, — This morning early we took our last
look at the beautiful Bay of Panama, which appeared
lovelier than ever in the beams of the rising sun.
Our ride this time was, if possible, even hotter than
when we traversed the same ground a month ago;
but the beauty of the forest scenery and luxuriance
of vegetation is still the same, and yet still new. The
railway being now completed as far as a little Indian
village called Rio Obispo, we were, by rather hastening
our mules and considerably heating ourselves, enabled
to perform the passage across in one day. We arrived
at Riô at half-past one P. M., having had a quick
broiling ride from Panama. I was partly amused
and partly shocked at the necessity of letting my
Guayaquil parrot be carried on the back of a negro
all this distance. The ground was absolutely scorch-
ing to the touch, yet the black bearer had bare feet.
He however did not seem to mind this, and trudged
on apparently contented. Not so poor " Lorita."

I am sorry to say she completely lost her temper and
every time her carrier hitched her cage up or down,
or otherwise deranged her equilibrium, she began to
swear most lustily all the bad words her Spanish
educational *repertoire* could furnish her.   Luckily
there will be few in England likely to understand her
if she should commit any similar misdemeanors
there, as besides her bad language being Spanish, it
is provincial, and has a great deal of dialect incomprehensible to the world in general.   We left Rio by
the train, and in three hours more we were once
again on board the Dee, where it was really pleasant
to find ourselves so heartily welcomed, and to see the
happy faces of the white people, and the grinning ones
of the blacks, as they all came crowding round us on
our arrival.

8th.—Early this morning the " Bonnie Dee " took
a run down to Chagres, a little bit of extra travel for
which I am by no means sorry, as it affords me an
opportunity of seeing a place now but rarely visited.
Chagres was formerly the starting-point for the people
bound across the isthmus; they here embarked in the
little canoes and generally spent three or four days
tedious poling up the river.   Now of course the
Navy Bay railroad has usurped all other modes of
transit.   I have seldom, however, been more pleased
with the appearance of a place than I was with this,
partly I suppose from the surprise.   I·had generally

figured Chagres to myself as a parched, sandy, unhealthy, and perfectly flat part of the world; instead
of which I found something as nearly as possible the
exact reverse of all this.   We landed from a beautiful little bay, quite land locked; and so calm and
still was everything around that we could almost have
fancied ourselves the first discoverers of the soil.   A
short walk however brought us to the town, so called,
of Chagres.   This consists merely of a few Indian
huts, the few establishments that once existed for the
temporary accommodation of travellers being now
either closed or entirely demolished, and the rest have
returned to their primitive simplicity.   We next
ascended the heights and visited the remains of the
old castle of Chagres, once a great stronghold of the
Spaniards, but now left to the mercies of weather
and time; a sad pity.   There are some splendid guns,
most elaborately carved and ornamented, but all deserted and left to their fate; also a cellar containing
no end of barrels of gunpowder, but all so damp that
a bonfire would fail to ignite them.   The view from
every side was most beautiful, and we left it much
regretting that time allowed us so short a visit.
Before re-embarking we were shown another and
different scene, but a most lovely one, a green valley
and a forest walk, with a clear bright stream rushing
at our feet, and, above all, the warm blue sky and that

indescribable stillness in the air so peculiar to these tropical climes, So farewell to Chagres. And now we are once more upon the waters. We returned to Navy Bay to take up the mails, and then finally took our departure.

9th and *10th.*—We have experienced a most violent gale of wind during these two days; moreover, it has been all the wrong way, or what sailors call right ahead. We were much rejoiced, therefore, to find ourselves this morning, the 11th, in the long creek, and consequently smooth water, leading to Cartagena, at which place we landed about eleven o'clock. Mr. Kortright, remembering that we had not been able to see anything of the place on our former visit, had very kindly sent his carriage to meet us, and although our time was still very limited, we had a very agreeable drive all about the environs of the city. We went to the fort of the Popa, and thus had an opportunity of examining it and its strange shape more nearly. The building which crowns its summit is a convent. We stopped often, to gather some of the beautiful flowers which grow in wild profusion all around. The town is handsome, and besides reminding me, as I before mentioned, of Venice in the distance, the narrow streets and overhanging roofs of the houses on a nearer view recalled Genoa to my recollection. About an hour ago we returned and partook of luncheon with our hospitable host. I am writing this from his house, so that it will bear the Cartagena post-mark. The time is drawing near now for going on board the Dee again, and to-night we shall take our last look at South America.

Ever your affectionate,

C.

CHAPTER XLV.

On board the Conway, off Porto Rico, March 18th. — My dear Father, — Since the date of my last letter until yesterday, we have had a regular succession of gales, almost amounting' to hurricane; the first really bad weather (for any length of time consecutively) that we have suffered since our arrival in the land of the West. We reached St. Thomas yesterday morning at eight o'clock. All things much the same there. Having transferred ourselves and our effects from the Dee to this vessel, we had about the time to make ourselves comfortable before sailing. We are now bound on our last island trip, Jamaica being our present destination. Early this morning we anchored in the harbour of Porto Rico, or I should more correctly say, St. Juan de Porto Rico, that being the name of the seaport. But a great disappointment has awaited us here. We are not allowed to land, vessels coming from St. Thomas being in quarantine, although the cholera has disappeared from there now. They think it

better to be on the safe side. We are therefore
obliged to rest contented with what we can see from
the ship of the town and harbour, which bear a
most striking resemblance to Havana, only on a
smaller scale. It was very pleasant at all events to
see the dear old Spanish flag again waving over the
walls, though I fear this will be the last occasion on
which we shall meet with it in this part of the world.
We shall leave here at sunset; I shall therefore
resume my letter at our next halting-place, which
will I believe be Hayti. Meanwhile it is no slight
comfort to have calm weather after the storms of
the past week. .   .   .   .

19th.—We arrived in the Bay of Jacmel this
morning, and landed immediately, as we were
allowed a short time to stay. The island is now
more generally called St. Domingo, than by its
original name of Hayti. Whence this has arisen I
know not, as St. Domingo was a town so called by
Christopher Columbus, the island having been first
discovered by him on Sunday; but up to very
recently it has been called indifferently Hispaniola
or Hayti. The appearance of Jacmel from a distance is more prepossessing then it proves to be on
a closer inspection. Of course I speak only of the
town, which seen from the sea looks Babylonian; that
is, laid out in terraces and hanging gardens, but turns
out really nothing of the sort, merely the accidental

grouping of some trees within the walls. The scenery around is, however, beautiful, as only the Antilles are. The French claim for Hayti, the same appellation as the Spanish do for Cuba, " La Reine des Antilles." Being here so short a time, and able only to take a very superficial view of it, I am of course unable to determine how far this may be merited. Still I cannot imagine it can equal Cuba, at least with its present semi-savage rulers. What it might be in Spanish hands, to whom it certainly legitimately belongs, is another question.* The Emperor Soulouque, the Duke of Marmalade, and the rest of his sugary suite are at Port-au-Prince, so we were not gratified with a sight of them. .　　.　　.

Kingston, Jamaica, March 22nd. — We landed here this morning only, though we arrived last evening, but too late to enter Port Royal harbour, which requires daylight, or at least bright moonlight. This is a pity, as I hear the view is fine approaching Port Royal from the south. We are not going to wait to see any sights here (if any exist) at present, but have engaged a carriage to take us to Spanish Town, about twelve miles off; whence I shall despatch this letter. .　. 3 P.M. we have just arrived here; had a very pleasant drive. There is a railroad

* While these pages are in the press, St. Domingo has actually returned to its old allegiance, and once again belongs to Spain. Is this the first act in the revival of the ancient glories of this once mighty monarchy ?

for the benefit of people in a hurry, but as we wished
to see a little of the country, we preferred the slower
mode of progress.   Our friends are staying in the
country, enjoying the mountain air ; but, fortunately
Sir Joshua Rowe had come into town this morning,
and so received us.   We are to accompany him to-
morrow to The Cedars, his mountain residence.
Adieu now.   This letter will go back by the return
steamer.   Ever your affectionate,

C.

CHAPTER XLVI.

The Cedars, March 29th. — My dear Father, — We have passed a very pleasant week among the hills; the scenery of Jamaica is certainly very beautiful, and I think grows upon one every day; at least I find it prettier and finer now than I did the first day. The verdure is perfectly wonderful, and the view from the lawn of The Cedars, of hill and valley all thickly covered with trees of every kind and every variety of tint, with Port Royal in the distance, and the sea bounding the horizon, form a landscape one could scarcely ever tire of gazing at. I think my chief admiration here in the way of trees and plants are the orange and lemon trees; they are quite lovely. They grow to a great height and in every direction, and with their profusion of golden fruit, snowy flowers, and dark glossy leaves, all in full bloom at the same time, make the orange, in my opinion, the queen of plants. There is a pretty place called Keith Hall a short distance from The Cedars; but higher up the hill side they command a more extensive view, and one particularly beautiful, of a chain of hills, and one especially called Monte Diablo.   I also observed some very fine specimens of bamboo trees; they are so very graceful and fairy-like.   There is a cluster of them on Sir Joshua Rowe's property that look exactly like a gigantic bunch of Prince of Wales' feathers.

31st.—We returned to town yesterday. To-day we paid a visit to Lady Barkly at Government House; then went over the courts of justice and the House of Assembly: nothing very remarkable in either. Matters seem in a very bad way in the house, and the Governor has a difficult and thankless part to play. Quarrels "never ending, still beginning," seem to be the only order of the day attended to vigorously in the Jamaican parliament. We went afterwards to the cathedral, where the principal object of attraction is the beautiful marble monument (by Baily) to Lady Elgin, who died in her youth and beauty here during Lord E.'s governorship of the island. The House of Assembly voted a sum of £300 for the sculpture, and the artist has been very successful, both in the resemblance of the statue to the original, and in the general design and execution of the whole.

April 4th.—Rode some days ago to a most romantic spot, though bearing a very uncouth name, "the Bog Walk:" without any exception, the love-

BOG WALK JAMAICA.

liest and yet the strangest bit of forest scenery I
have met with in my wanderings. The principal
features in the landscape are the bamboo trees, and
on entering the particular glade called the "bog,"
a most wondrous spectacle is presented to the view;
the graceful branches of the bamboos, of which I
have before spoken, by some curious *fantaisie* of
nature, have entwined themselves and interlaced
each other over your head. The effect is a perfect
gothic arch, and as it is repeated and continuous
for a very considerable distance, one might fancy
oneself in the "long drawn aisle and fretted vault"
of some old cathedral. In the middle of this aisle
or avenue rushes a clear, bright, noisy stream, dashing
turbulently against stones, rocks, and other obstacles
that come in its way. Between this stream and
the stems of the beautiful arches there is just room
for a horse and his rider to pass. The name of
"the Bog Walk" is, I hear, an English corruption
of "La Boca," or some say, "La Boca de Aqua,"
meaning the mouth or river's mouth; the little
stream I have mentioned being near the mouth of
one of Jamaica's many rivers. The island is greatly
famed for the number and variety of its woods.
Many were pointed out in our ride to day, mahogany,
satin wood, ebony, lignum vitæ, &c.

7th.—Left Sir J. and Lady Rowe for an excursion
of a few days in the mountains. Drove from Spanish

Town to the terminus, and thence by the railway to Kingston. We had here a fine view of all the shipping in this harbour, as well as in Port Royal. In the latter is the quarantine ground; we noticed a good number of victimised ships bearing the unlucky yellow flag. It is peculiarly unfortunate to be detained here in quarantine, as Port Royal and Kingston are considered the most, if not the only, unhealthy parts of the island.

Hence we started for Newcastle, a distance of fourteen miles, passing through "Up Park Camp" on our way. This is a military station containing a force varying from 300 to 500 men, according to circumstances. During times of cholera, fever, or any other trouble, Up Park is considered generally to possess purer and healthier air than any on the coast. About eleven miles from Kingston we arrived at a place called the Botanical Garden. Once upon a time a garden did really exist; now there is but the name. It is the limit to which ordinary shaped carriages have access; beyond it either two wheeled vehicles, such as volantes, or gigs, or very narrow carts, are the only means of passage by draught. We rode on horseback, my old friend Col. Luxmoore (who by a curious coincidence commands the detachment of the 16th Regiment now at Newcastle) having sent saddle horses for our use. We had a pleasant and very picturesque ride during the remainder of the distance, and arrived at Col. L.'s quarters just as the day was fading; found Mrs. Luxmoore and my friend Cissy (her daughter) waiting to welcome me. An hour after this we sat down to a merry dinner, consisting chiefly of former friends and acquaintances. The last time we met having been in Greece, we little anticipated the change of scene four years would produce.

8*th*.—This is the funniest little nook in the world; there is scarcely an inch of level ground to be discovered far or near. The houses or cottages used by the officers as quarters are scattered about in every direction, above and below, some of them perched so high as to be very difficult of access. The garden belonging to this cottage of Col. L.'s where we are is some forty feet above us; all the dwelling-places have this nest-like appearance. In this garden, which when arrived at is remarkably pretty, grows a natural curiosity, in the existence of which I certainly should not have believed had I not actually seen it; namely, a *green rose*. There were three blossoming on the bush, besides several buds. The flowers were in all respects like the ordinary pink, red, or white rose, the same soft velvety leaves, only of a pale green colour; in all other particulars the plant was just like any other, the stalks, thorns, green leaves, &c. I was allowed to gather one of the three blossoms I had seen in flower, and have placed it between the leaves of this book; not that I shall expect any one who may see it hereafter in its faded hue to believe in its original one, unless they too should have visited Newcastle and Col. Luxmoore's garden. I shall close this letter now, or it will be too voluminous.

Ever your affectionate,

C.

CHAPTER XLVII.

Newcastle, Jamaica, April 10*th.*—My dear Father, —We made an excursion on horseback the day before yesterday to the St. Katharine hills. They are off-shoots from the Blue Mountain chain. One might well fancy oneself in Scotland, or, I should perhaps rather say, in Wales. The keen cold air (we are about 4000 feet above the sea), the smooth green grass covered hills, bear a great resemblance to the scenery of some of our excursions among the Welsh mountains and valleys. This, however, though very healthy and beneficial to the troops after being baked in Kingston, is the least pleasant and least pretty expedition I have yet made. It is too bleak and too poor looking to be appreciated after the warmth and the luxuriant vegetation we have so lately left. Next day we made a far more agreeable excursion to Charlottenberg, the country residence of the Bishop of Jamaica. I have rarely been so strongly tempted to break the tenth commandment as I was on entering this delightful abode ; that it belongs to a Bishop, too,

o

makes the enormity of my coveting worse still. I
thoroughly realised on this spot the poet's apostro-
phe to a yet very different scene.

"A blending of all beauties; streams and dells,
    Fruit, foliage, crag, wood, mountain, cornfield"—

the last word must here be omitted as the " *vine* " is
not one of the blended beauties in this fair scene.
Grapes do exist nevertheless in Jamaica, and are ex-
cellent-flavoured; but the vine is not a distinctive
feature or characteristic of the country. It would
be difficult to single out any one particular class of
tree or plant in the rich and varied tract of country,
spread before us to-day, as an especial object of admiration. When you have mangoes, cocoa-nuts,
allspice (pimento), olives, tamarinds, banana, oranges,
pomegranates, sugar, and coffee, all growing in luxuriant profusion around, you are too much dazzled
with the whole to be able to specify what is the most
beautiful. At least I found it so. Then besides the
wonderful scene of fertility I have been trying to
describe, the magnificence of the view can scarcely
be imagined from the terrace of Charlottenberg,
backed by the noble range of the Blue Mountains,
and bounded at the horizon by the azure coloured
sea. The house is in perfect keeping with the
gardens and other external belongings of the Bishop.
The rooms are spacious and cool. The floors beau-

tifully inlaid with specimens of the various woods
grown in Jamaica; tables, chairs, and other furniture of carved ebony.   Having visited the principal
rooms, we proceeded to a little summer house, where
we took some refreshment, and gazed once more at
the enchanting view beneath us, through the medium
of stained glass of different colours, which is let in here
and there in the windows. To-morrow we are to set out
on the last expedition of any consequence we shall
make in this part of the world ; namely, we purpose
making the ascent of the Blue Mountain Peak.   The
difficulties are great, I hear, and some of our friends
think the undertaking very hazardous. On the other
hand, I am told that with good courage and good
will to persevere, we can do it; and that, moreover, Lord Metcalfe went up when he was an old
man, and suffering from the gout; so under these
circumstances I think there can be scarcely any unconquerable difficulties for us.   The actual height is
nothing particular, merely 8000 feet, yet I understand
the chief actual inconvenience one suffers is from the
excessive rarity of the air, and the consequent
difficulty of breathing.   I shall be glad, however, if
we should be ultimately successful, and reach the top
without any hindrance, as among other objects to be
attained, is a sight of dear old Cuba, which will
much rejoice me to behold once more, before taking
my departure from the west.

11th.—We left Newcastle on horseback about 10 o'clock A.M. Our destination this evening being the house of a Mr. Pownall, who resides at the foot of the mountain, having come here many years ago, and lived at his present abode ever since. From his house I am now writing this. We passed over a considerable part of the country to-day, which we saw yesterday from Charlottenberg. Found a close examination as beautiful in its way as the more distant one. The coffee plantations especially gain on a near approach; the perfume is delicious, and the plant, whether in the flower or berry, is graceful and pretty. An extensive estate, part of which we traversed, was pointed out to me as having formed a portion of the Duke of Buckingham's property in this island. We reached Mr. P.'s "hermitage" about 3 o'clock, and were welcomed by him with much civility. It is a curious fancy that has led this gentleman here. I understand he was formerly a farmer, and lived in Essex (rather a contrast to the Blue Mountain). Some accidental circumstance having caused him to pay a visit to Jamaica, here he has remained ever since, and has farmed his little tropical estate very successfully. He calls himself "the old man of the mountain," of which for many years past he has done the honours to all comers. We sat down to dinner shortly after our arrival, a plentiful repast in the English style. A "distin-

guished dish," to my great amusement, being broad
beans and bacon.   Our host thinks we may safely try
the experiment to-morrow morning, and he proposes
to accompany us as well as our present party, and
the regular guides.   It seems the grand difficulty to
be conquered, is a place commonly called "Jacob's
Ladder," which people ascend as they can, there
being no steps and no path, and only at rare intervals any *terra firma* on which to plant the feet.   This
does not sound pleasant; but we shall see what to-
morrow will bring.   Our meal being ended, we
strolled out to look at the coffee garden attached to
the house.   The trees are now in full bloom, of a
pale pink colour.   The odour is most agreeable, very
aromatic.   This is a very small plantation, Mr. P.
farming it for his own private use, as I suppose he
would *turnips* in his native Essex.   What a difference !

12th.— Well, the Peak is a *fait accompli*, and we
are alive to tell the tale; but it is an undertaking I
should be very sorry to attempt again, and one I
should not have pursued now to the end, had it been
practicable to return; but this was impossible.   I will
presently say why.

We started betimes in the morning, a party of
five besides the guides.   For about two miles and a
half we rode on ponies; and this, though comparatively easy work to the rest of the journey, was in

itself rather dangerous; at least we ran the risk of
our faces and features being disfigured several times.
A kind of track, it can scarcely be termed a path or
road, has been cut through the dense tangled masses
of vegetation with which the sides of the mountain
are clothed; but as the visits of strangers to the
Peak are few and far between, the prolific soil allows
of considerable growth of branches, leaves, and
parasite creepers of all descriptions in the intervals
between the times of cutting the track. To day, as
we were all obliged to advance in single file, and our
ponies were chiefly anxious to follow each other
without troubling themselves about their riders, we
were repeatedly caught, sometimes across the eyes,
sometimes across the mouth, and last and worst,
under the chin, narrowly escaping strangulation, by
the boughs and tendrils of the trees and their parasites, interlacing each other across our path. For
my own part I speedily found my only chance of
safety lay in leaving my pony to his own devices,
and providing for myself as well as I could. So,
quickly twisting my bridle round the pommel, I laid
myself as flat down as I could, on the neck of my
gallant steed, and extended my legs towards his tail;
and in this interesting Mazeppa-like attitude (which
would have made my fortune at Astley's) was accomplished the remainder of the equestrian portion
of our course. We now had to proceed on foot, and

for about a mile or so we found the ascent no very
formidable task — stumbling over the stumps of old
trees, and entangling oneself in briars, being the
worst catastrophes to speak of. Soon, however, occurred a change, of which the first symptom was
want of breath, and a necessity of stopping every
few steps, to try and recover it. The cold, too, now
became intense. Just before reaching the terrible
Jacob's Ladder, at a sudden turn of the path, a
splendid view burst upon our sight, and with which
I heartily wish we had contented ourselves, and
advanced no further. From the pinnacle on which
we were perched, we seemed to look straight down
several thousand feet, and where the orange trees
apparently dipped their branches into the clear bright
waves beneath. This, however, was an optical delusion — the projection of the land giving the branches
the appearance of touching the water, though in
reality some hundred feet above it. Finally, at the
edge of the horizon could be just faintly traced the
outline of the Cuban coast, and the highland near
Sant Jago de Cuba. I understand now whence the
name of Jacob's Ladder is derived. This is to all
intents and purposes a road through the air, the
mode of progress being catching hold of branches of
trees, and by their means swinging or hoisting yourself up, till you find a resting place, or perch for the
sole of your foot, on some bough or stump, and so

on *ad infinitum.* For a few yards we got on tolerably, though the fatigue was something beyond conception, for it is scarcely ever possible to be helped by any other person, as each one is generally on a different level. I would have gladly now abandoned the project, but to retrace one's steps on Jacob's Ladder, is an impossibility. One may get up, one cannot get down these aerial steps. Exhaustion, cold, and the painful gasping for breath, from which we were now suffering, made it very problematical whether we could move another step. Brandy and milk (a curious concoction) was now administered, at least so it was said to be; but I was past all power of tasting, or even of knowing any thing crossed my lips. I can only suppose the instinct of self-preservation impelled us onwards, as we did eventually reach the summit. Here I must have lost all consciousness, for on coming to myself, I found I was seated on the ground, in a little log hut, before a blazing fire; two people chafing my hands, which were turned almost slate colour, and a third trying to insinuate a glass of wine between my lips, which they informed me were of the same beautiful hue. E. told me she had been in much the same plight, but had recovered more quickly. The shelter from the keen air, and the cheerful warmth of the fire, gradually restored us to our natural feelings and complexions, and then we were not long in discovering that we were in a state bordering on starvation ; so we very soon set to, with right good will, to demolish the excellent luncheon our host had provided. We then proceeded to look at the prospect we had incurred such hardships in trying to see. I was not a little provoked at finding it in nearly all respects the same as we had enjoyed at the *foot* of Jacob's Ladder. Soon after this we commenced the descent, but not by the same route. I should have thought we might have gone up by the road we came down, but they tell me it would have been impossible, so I take it upon trust, as I certainly shall not make the experiment. We reached the hermitage safely, though terribly tired.

13th. — Much refreshed from a good long night's rest. Said good-bye to the hermit, and rode back to Newcastle, where we found our friends much astonished to hear we had actually accomplished the ascent, they having believed we should take alarm at the last moment.

20th, St. Thomas. — We sail for England at midnight. Since writing the foregoing last pages we returned to Spanish Town and were enabled to spend two pleasant days with Sir J. and Lady Rowe, whom we left with much regret. This is the fifth visit we have paid to St. Thomas since we left home. Still, in my opinion, it is as pretty and as green as ever. I shall always keep a kindly remembrance of it, and

think of it as of an old friend.   Our long and varied
journey is now drawing to its close.   Between this
and England it is scarcely probable anything worth
chronicling will arise.   We have bid farewell to the
many friends and companions of our voyages, a sor-
rowful enough task, only brightened by anticipations
of the future, and, on my side, of seeing you and
home again.

Till then adieu, .

Your ever affectionate daughter,

CLARA FITZROY PALEY.

April, 1854.

ENVOI.

WHETHER it may ever be my lot to revisit the sunny land I have endeavoured to paint in the foregoing pages I know not. I parted from it with much regret, and shall ever bear the grateful recollection that the year I spent on the other side of the Atlantic was the happiest and most peaceful period of my life, from the days of childhood until the present time.

CLARA FITZROY BROMLEY.

September, 1855.

THE END.

66, Brook Street, Hanover Square, W.

MESSRS. SAUNDERS, OTLEY, & CO.'s
LITERARY ANNOUNCEMENTS.

~~~~~~~~~~~~~~~~~~~

THE VOYAGE OF THE NOVARA ROUND
THE WORLD. The Circumnavigation of the Globe, by the Austrian
Frigate Novara. English Edition. Containing an Unpublished Letter
from Baron Humboldt. With numerous wood engravings. Dedicated,
by special permission, to Sir Roderick Murchison. 3 vols., 8vo.

THE MARQUIS OF DALHOUSIE'S ADMINIS-
TRATION of BRITISH INDIA. By Edwin Arnold, M.A., of University College, Oxford.

THE POLITICAL LIFE of the EARL of DERBY.

THE LIFE of the RIGHT HON. BENJAMIN
DISRAELI, M.P.

THE LIVES of the SPEAKERS of the HOUSE of
COMMONS. By William Nathaniel Massey, Esq., M.P., author of
" The History of England," and Chairman of Ways and Means.

THE LATITUDINARIANS.
A Chapter of Church History, from the Accession of Archbishop Tillot-
son in 1691, to the Death of Archdeacon Blackburne, in 1787. By
Edward Churton, M.A., Archdeacon of Cleveland.

THE LIFE OF THE RIGHT HON. W. E.
GLADSTONE, M.P. 1 vol., 8vo.

The FINANCIAL POLICY OF ENGLAND
for Twenty Years, from 1842 to 1861. By Sir Stafford Northcote,
Bart., M.P.

The RELATION OF CHURCH AND STATE,
and the Nature and Effects of an Established Religion. By Lord Robert
Montagu, M.P.

The HISTORY of the CHURCH,
The Low Church, and the Broad Church Parties. By the Venerable
Archdeacon Denison.

The LIFE and CORRESPONDENCE of LORD
BACON ; an Answer to Mr. Hepworth Dixon's " Personal History of
Bacon." By a Member of the Middle Temple.

ECCLESIA RESTITUTA.
By F. C. Massingberd, M.A., Prebendary of Lincoln and Rector of
Ormsby.

SEVEN ANSWERS to the 'ESSAYS and REVIEWS,'
BY SEVEN WRITERS IN SEVEN SEPARATE ESSAYS.

THE HISTORY OF THE CONSERVATIVE
PARTY, from the Defection of Sir Robert Peel to the Present Time.
1 vol., 8vo.

THE HISTORY OF THE CHURCH OF
ENGLAND, from the Death of Elizabeth to the Present Time. By
the Rev. Geo. G. Perry, M.A., Rector of Waddington, late Fellow and
Tutor of Lincoln College, Oxford. 3 vols., 8vo.

CHURCH RATE A NATIONAL TRUST.
By the Venerable Archdeacon Denison. 1 vol., 8vo, 10s. 6d.

THE CHURCHES OF THE EAST.
By the Rev. George Williams, B.D., Senior Fellow of King's College,
Cambridge. 1 vol., 8vo.

THE AMERICAN CHURCH and the AMERICAN
UNION. By Henry Caswall, D.D., of Trinity College, Connecticut, and
Prebendary of Sarum. 1 v., post 8vo.

PHILOSOPHY ; or, THE SCIENCE of TRUTH,
being a Treatise on First Principles, Mental, Physical, and Verbal. By
James Haig, Esq., M.A., of Lincoln's Inn.

RECOLLECTIONS OF GENERAL GARI-
BALDI; or, TRAVELS FROM ROME TO LUCERNE, comprising
a Visit to the Mediterranean Islands of La Madalena and Caprera,
and the Home of General Garibaldi. 1 vol. 10s. 6d.

THE TRAVELS AND ADVENTURES OF
DR. WOLFF, the Bokhara Missionary. New and cheap edition, revised
throughout, with full length Portrait, 12s.

AN AUTUMN TOUR IN SPAIN.
By the Rev. R. Roberts, B.A., of Trinity College, Cambridge, and
Vicar of Milton Abbas. With numerous Engravings. 21s.

HISTORICAL MEMOIRS OF THE
SUCCESSORS OF ST. PATRICK AND ARCHBISHOPS OF
ARMAGH. By James Henthorne Todd, D.D., F.S.A., President of
the Royal Irish Academy, Treasurer of St. Patrick's Cathedral, Regius
Professor of Hebrew in the University, and Senior Fellow of Trinity
College, Dublin. 2 vols., 8vo.

The GOVERNING MINDS of IRELAND.

The COURT of NAPLES in OUR OWN TIMES.

A WOMAN'S WANDERINGS in the WESTERN
WORLD. Letters to Sir Fitzroy Kelly, from his Daughter.

THE LIFE OF GEORGE FOX,
The Founder of the Quakers. From numerous original sources. 10s. 6d.

RECOLLECTIONS of AN ATTORNEY. 10s. 6d.

THE PRIVATE JOURNAL
OF THE MARQUESS OF HASTINGS, Governor-General and Commander-in-Chief in India.
Edited by his Daughter, SOPHIA, the Marchioness of Bute. Second Edition, 2 vols. post 8vo, with Map and Index. 21s.

AN ANSWER to 'ESSAYS and REVIEWS.'
By Canon Woodgate.

NAPOLEON THE THIRD ON ENGLAND.
Selections from his own writings. Translated by J. H. SIMPSON. 5s.

THE HUNTING GROUNDS OF THE OLD
WORLD. By H. A. L. (the Old Shekarry). Second Edition. 21s.

HIGHLANDS AND HIGHLANDERS;
As they were and as they are. By WILLIAM GRANT STEWART. First and Second series, price 5s. each; extra bound, 6s. 6d.

THE ENGLISHMAN IN CHINA.
With numerous Woodcuts. 10s. 6d.

LECTURES ON THE EPISTLE TO THE
EPHESIANS. By the Rev. R. J. M'GHEE. Second Edition. 2 vols, Reduced price, 15s.

PRE-ADAMITE MAN; or,
THE STORY OF OUR OLD PLANET AND ITS INHABITANTS, TOLD BY SCRIPTURE AND SCIENCE. Beautifully Illustrated by Hervieu, Dalziel Brothers, &c. 1 vol, post 8vo, 10s. 6d.

LOUIS CHARLES DE BOURBON:
THE "¶PRISONER OF THE TEMPLE." 3s.

A HANDY-BOOK FOR RIFLE VOLUNTEERS.
With 14 Coloured Plates and Diagrams. By Captain W. G. Hartley, author of "A New System of Drill." 7s. 6d.

RECOLLECTIONS of a WINTER CAMPAIGN
IN INDIA, in 1857—58. By CAPTAIN OLIVER J. JONES, R.N. With numerous illustrations drawn on stone by Day, from the Author's Sketches. In 1 vol. royal 8vo, 16s.

TWO YEARS IN SYRIA.
By T. Lewis Farley, Esq., Late Chief Accountant of the Ottoman Bank, Beyrout. 12s. Second Edition.

DIARY OF TRAVELS IN THREE QUARTERS
OF THE GLOBE. By an Australian Settler. 2 vols, post 8vo, 21s.

The NEW SPEAKER.

The TEN COMMANDMENTS.
By the Rev. J. McCaul.

MOUNT LEBANON AND ITS INHABITANTS:
A Ten Years' Residence from 1842 to 1852. By Colonel Churchill, Staff Officer in the British Expedition to Syria. Second Edition. 3 vols, 8vo, £1 5s.

FROM SOUTHAMPTON TO CALCUTTA.
Sketches of Anglo-Indian Life. 10s. 6d.

THE TABLETTE BOOKE of LADYE MARY
KEYES, OWNE SISTER TO THE MISFORTUNATE LADYE JANE DUDLIE. Post 8vo, 10s. 6d.

TRAVEL and RECOLLECTIONS of TRAVEL.
By Dr. John Shaw. 1 vol, post 8vo, 7s. 6d.

LETTERS ON INDIA.
By Edward Sullivan, Esq., Author of 'Rambles in North and South America;' 'The Bungalow and the Tent;' 'From Boulogne to Babel Mandeb;' 'A Trip to the Trenches;' &c. 1 vol. 7s.

CAMPAIGNING IN KAFFIRLAND; or,
SCENES AND ADVENTURES IN THE KAFFIR WAR OF 1851—52. By Captain W. R. King. Second Edition. 1 vol. 8vo, 14s.

THE RELIGIOUS TENDENCIES OF THE
AGE. 6s. 6d.

ADVENTURES OF A GENTLEMAN
IN SEARCH OF A HORSE. By Sir George Stephen. With illustrations by Cruikshank. New and cheaper Edition, 5s.

THE LANGUAGE OF FLOWERS,
Elegant Gift Book for the Season. Beautifully bound in green watered silk, with coloured plates. Containing the Art of Conveying Sentiments of Esteem and Affection. Eleventh edition, dedicated, by permission, to the late Duchess of Kent. 10s. 6d.

THE MANAGEMENT OF BEES;
With a description of the "Ladies' Safety Hive." By Samuel Bagster, Jun. 1 vol., illustrated. 7s.

THE HANDBOOK OF TURNING,
With numerous plates. A complete and Practical Guide to the Beautiful Science of Turning in all its Branches. 1 vol. 7s. 6d.

TEXTS FOR TALKERS.
By FRANK FOWLER. 3s. 6d.

THE SUMMER TOUR of an INVALID. 5s. 6d.

ARMY MISRULE: BARRACK THOUGHTS.
By a COMMON SOLDIER. 3s.

Fiction.

WHY PAUL FERROLL KILLED HIS WIFE.
By the Author of " Paul Ferroll." Third Edition. 10s. 6d.

OUR NEW RECTOR.
Edited by the Author of ' Mr. Verdant Green.' 10s. 6d.

THE RECTOR'S DAUGHTERS.
A Tale of Clerical Life. 10s. 6d.

SWEETHEARTS AND WIVES.
A Novel. By MARGUERITE A. POWER. 3 vols., 31s. 6d.

AN M.P. IN SEARCH OF A CREED.
A Novel. 10s. 6d.

ROTTEN ROW. A Novel. 2 vols., 21s.

CRISPIN KEN. By the Author of ' Miriam May.'
Dedicated, by special permission, to the Right Hon. Sir E. B. Lytton, Bart., M.P. 2 vols., 21s. Second Edition.

WHO SHALL BE DUCHESS? or,
THE NEW LORD OF BURLEIGH. A Novel. 2 vols., 21s.

THE LIGHTHOUSE. A Novel. 2 vols., 21s.

THE SKELETON IN THE CUPBOARD.
By Lady Scott. 2 vols., 21s. Cheaper Edition, 5s.

TOO LATE! By Mrs. DIMSDALE. 7s. 6d.

HELEN. A Romance of Real Life. 7s. 6d.

THE CASTLE and the COTTAGE in SPAIN.
By Lady Wallace, Author of ' Clara; or, Slave Life in Europe.' 2 vols., 21s.

CYRUS. By Lady Julia Lockwood.

GERTRUDE MELTON; or,
NATURE'S NOBLEMAN. A Tale. 7s. 6d.

RUTH BAYNARD'S STORY. 1 vol., 10s. 6d.

The LADY of the MANOR of TOPCROFT. 21s.

EDMONDALE.

LOVING and BEING LOVED.
By the authoress of "Zingra, the Gipsy."

VANITY CHURCH. 2 vols., 21s.

MY WIFE'S PINMONEY.
By E. E. NELSON, a grand niece of the great Lord Nelson. 5s.

THE EMIGRANT'S DAUGHTER.
Dedicated, by permission, to the Empress of Russia. 5s.

MIRIAM MAY. 4th Edition. 10s. 6d.

WHISPERING VOICES OF THE YULE.
Tales for Christmas. 5s.

THE SENIOR FELLOW.
A Tale of Clerical Life. 10s. 6d.

ALMACK'S.
A Novel. Dedicated to the Ladies Patronesses of the Balls at Almack's.
New Edition, 1 vol, crown 8vo, 10s. 6d.

NELLY CAREW.
By MISS POWER. 2 vols, 21s.

MEMOIRS OF A LADY IN WAITING.
By the Author of 'Adventures of Mrs. Colonel Somerset in Caffraria.'
2 vols, 18s.

HULSE HOUSE.
A Novel. By the Author of 'Anne Gray.' 2 vols. post 8vo, 21s.

THE NEVILLES OF GARRETSTOWN.
A Historical Tale. Edited, and with a Preface by the Author of
'Emilia Wyndham.' 3 vols, post 8vo, 31s. 6d.

CORVODA ABBEY.
A Tale. 1 vol, post 8vo, 10s. 6d.

THE VICAR OF LYSSEL.
The Diary of a Clergyman in the 18th century. 4s. 6d.

GOETHE IN STRASBOURG.
A Dramatic Nouvelette. By H. Noel Humphreys. 7s. 6d.

SQUIRES AND PARSONS.
A Church Novel. 1 vol. 10s. 6d.

THE DEAN ; or, the POPULAR PREACHER.
By BERKELEY AIKIN, Author of 'Anne Sherwood.' 3 vols. post 8vo.
31s. 6d.

CHARLEY NUGENT ; or,
PASSAGES IN THE LIFE OF A SUB. A Novel, 3 vols, post 8vo.
31s. 6d.

ADRIFT.
By Frank Fowler. Dedicated, by permission, to the Right Hon. B. Disraeli.

ASHCOMBE CHURCHYARD.

GREAT CATCHES and GREAT MATCHES.

SIDE WINDS.

PAUL FERROLL.
By the Author of ' IX Poems by V.' Fourth Edition. Post 8vo, 10s. 6d.

LORD AUBREY ; or,
WHAT SHALL I DO? By the Author of ' Every Day.' A Novel. 2 vols , 21s.

THE IRONSIDES.
A Tale of the English Commonwealth. 3 vols., 31s. 6d.

AGNES HOME. A Novel. 10s. 6d.

LA CAVA ; or,
RECOLLECTIONS OF THE NEAPOLITANS. 10s. 6d.

ANSELMO.
A Tale of Modern Italy. 2 vols., 21s.

THE DALRYMPLES ; or,
LONG CREDIT AND LONG CLOTH. 10s. 6d.

INSTINCT ; or, REASON.
By Lady JULIA LOCKWOOD. 5s. 6d.

CARELADEN HOUSE. A Novel. 10s. 6d.

Poetry.

Sir E. L. Bulwer Lytton's Eva,
AND OTHER POEMS.

Sacred Poems.
By the late Right Hon. Sir Robert Grant, with a Notice by Lord Glenelg.

Eustace ;
An Elegy. By the Right Hon. Charles Tennyson D'Eyncourt.

Oberon's Empire.
A Mask.

The Shadow of the Yew,
AND OTHER POEMS. By Norman B. Yonge,

Esther ;
And other Sacred Pieces. By the Rev. Charles B. GreatRex.